YOUTH SOCCER COACHING

McDonald's
Family Enclosure

YOUTH SOCCER COACHING

A COMPLETE GUIDE TO BUILDING A SUCCESSFUL TEAM

TONY CARR
WEST HAM UNITED YOUTH TEAM MANAGER
AND STUART PROSSOR

WARD LOCK

To all the Carr family, especially mum and dad, Kit and Charlie, for encouraging me – and paying for my FA full-licence coaching course when I was 20.

Tony Carr

To mum and dad, Anna and Imogen, for all their love, and to my friend Adam George – you'll always be missed.

Stuart Prossor

A WARD LOCK BOOK

First published in the UK 1997 by Ward Lock
Wellington House, 125 Strand
LONDON WC2R OBB

A Cassell Imprint

Black and white photography by Simon Pattle of the Training and Consultancy Company of the University of East London, Longbridge Road, Dagenham, Essex RM8 2AS

Distributed in the United States by Sterling Publishing Co., Inc.
387 Park Avenue South, New York, NY 10016–8810

A British Library Cataloguing in Publication Data block for this book may be obtained from the British Library

ISBN 0 7063 7578 5

Illustrations by Ethan Danielson
Book design by Richard Carr
Cover design by Jamie Tanner
Photographs on pages 15, 17, 19, 21, 22, 23, 27, 28 and 29 supplied by Colorsport
Printed and bound in Great Britain by Hillman Printers (Frome) Ltd

CONTENTS

ACKNOWLEDGEMENTS

Tony Carr would like to thank:
The Carr family (Brenda, Dean, Neil and Louise) for putting up with me during long hours of research; the West Ham United Board of Directors: Terry Brown (Chairman), Martin Cearns (Vice-Chairman), Charles Warner, Peter Storrie (Managing Director); Harry Redknapp and Frank Lampard, for their support; the managers I have been privileged to work under: Ron Greenwood, John Lyall, Lou Macari, Billy Bonds and Harry Redknapp; Ron Boyce, for being a positive influence, coaching colleague and good friend; Stan Burke, Jimmy Frith and Dave Gladstone, for their friendship and loyalty in working with the youth squad; Paul Heffer, Dave Bickles, Steve Twidell, Dave Knowles, Dean Wells and Peter Brabrook, for all their efforts in the schoolboy coaching department; Jimmy Hampson, for his tireless working in the youth scouting department; Sue Banks, for her patience and typing; the numerous youth players I have worked with, too many to mention, and those who appear in the photographs; in particular Dave Richardson (Youth Director, FA Premier League), Paul Ince (West Ham United, Manchester United, Inter Milan and England), Tony Cottee (West Ham United and England), Steve Potts (Captain, West Ham United); Trevor Brooking, for the Foreword; Steve Bacon, for photographs; Eddie Gillam, for supplying all the kit requirements; Shirley Austin, for endless cups of tea, Simon Pattle (University of East London), who took the photographs and advised with the artworks; A.D.W., for helping me find work when I needed it; Deborah Taylor, my commissioning editor at Cassell, who has been so enthusiastic about the publication of this book; and, last but not least, my great friends Keith and Jasmine Cosby, for their continuing support and friendship.

Stuart Prossor would like to thank:
His parents, Bob and Ingrid Prossor, for their love and wonderful support for this project; his sister, Anna, and niece, Imogen Wizz, for their love; Geoff Bird, for being a wonderful friend, but more particularly for assuming the role of personal editor and spending many hours reading the text and offering advice and help; Christine Bird, for her friendship and computer knowledge; Peter Littlewood, for his great friendship, loyalty and, above all, real belief in this project; Ken Dugdale, for his continued loyalty and support; Kevin Romijn and Bill Bradley, for being good friends and coaching colleagues; Simon George, a loyal friend, who will be a good coach one day; Steve Haslam, for being such an inspiration; the Long family of Kevin, Lorraine, Peter, Katrina and Michelle, for always being there; Margaret and Richard Martin, who kindly have me to stay when I visit London; Eric Batty, a football genius, who sadly is no longer with us, and Michael Jesset Snr, for his continuing support.

SOUTH EASTERN ELECTRICAL PLC
081- 506 1717
LONGLIFE
TEL:0171-537
PONY
PONY
LJK
FOR SALES SERVICE BODYSHOP
PARTS CALL0181-500 1090
CARLING

FOREWORD

Tony Carr and I played together in West Ham's Youth Team back in the early '60s and were extremely fortunate to come under the influence of two outstanding coaches – Ron Greenwood and John Lyall. Their training methods and philosophy created and reinforced West Ham's renowned reputation for playing entertaining and skilful football. I enjoyed myself so much I stayed at the club throughout my 19-year playing career. Tony's playing days were cut short by injury, but he was quickly persuaded to retain his close ties with the club, and to continue to develop the up-and-coming stars of the future.

I joined West Ham in 1965, just after they had won the European Cup Winners' Cup, following their FA Cup success the previous year. World Cup glory was to come in 1966, and the Hammers trio of Bobby Moore, Geoff Hurst and Martin Peters were to play a prominent part in the historic campaign. West Ham's style of play required all team members to have the basic skills of good control which naturally included the right kicking and passing techniques.

Youngsters today have far greater distractions and alternatives to football, which means we must make significant changes if our national game is not to languish behind the rest. It is these basic skills that have suffered more than anything since my younger days, as now football must compete with television, videos, computer games and numerous alternative sports. Although individuals can be born with natural skills, it is only regular practice that provides the necessary technique to play the game well. I believe the younger you start, the better. The years from the ages of five to eight are absolutely vital because youngsters are totally receptive to everything you tell them, and they have not developed any bad habits. They can be taught the correct techniques for kicking and control, while also being encouraged to use both feet.

Early football experience, during the primary school period up to the age of 11, is another crucial period. Throughout this time the emphasis should be placed on football being fun and something to be enjoyed. Unfortunately, a good deal of the junior football played in this age group is not undertaken by schools but by well-meaning parents. Too much emphasis is placed on winning at all costs, and quite frequently the 'shouts' from the sidelines are more of a hindrance than a help. Youngsters do make mistakes, which sometimes cost goals, but at that age they are on a learning curve and should not have their spirit and enthusiasm extinguished.

Once they move into the secondary school stage, the basic skills of control and passing should be strongly embedded. At the moment that is far from the case and too much time is still wasted in rectifying these problems which should be solved much earlier. Almost every training session I took part in at West Ham over 19 years involved working with a football. Even if it was a physical running session, it was quite often with a ball at our feet, so that our feel and comfort in possession was fully developed.

I cannot emphasize enough the importance of the word 'practice'. Improvement in skill does not just happen, and is unlikely to emerge just by playing matches because then there is a tendency not to try anything different. The ability to experiment and produce something unusual is perfected on a training pitch, before the players are confident enough to introduce it into a match. The more that these skills become habit, the happier the player becomes in expressing them in a game situation.

Tony has a huge wealth of coaching knowledge about small-sided groups and practices. I am an advocate of quality coaching at a very young age and believe a book of this sort should certainly prove invaluable in helping those all-important team managers make training more interesting, and also help them to put the fun factor back into our game. If that happens, a better prepared generation of footballers will emerge. My only last condition is that West Ham have first choice from the best! Good luck.

INTRODUCTION

IN FEBRUARY 1986, I began going to West Ham United's Chadwell Heath training ground. At that time John Lyall was manager of the prestigious London club and I regularly watched him and Tony Carr work. A quick telephone call was enough to join training for the day, and members of the coaching staff were always very friendly and accommodating towards anyone interested in the technical side of the game.

At the time, I noted the lack of a book or manual full of good ideas for coaches, particularly those working with youngsters who were aiming to produce quality players to play quality football. *Youth Soccer Coaching* is the product of this thought, and of the time I have spent over the last ten years visiting a variety of professional training grounds and watching coaches work.

From the outset, I realized that to write a book on coaching I would need the assistance of a world-class practitioner. Tony Carr, who is a truly outstanding coach, fitted the bill perfectly, and I therefore became a fly-on-the-wall at the training ground every day for a full three months, watching him and his West Ham colleagues at work.

Such is the simplicity and quality of the work that Tony does with his Youth Team, and its effectiveness in refining techniques and skills, that it may be transferred to all levels of the game – so this book can be used by coaches working in all kinds of situations, all around the world. It also aims to cover most facets of the game, with the exception of goal-keeping (an area for which most professional clubs employ a specialist coach). The book therefore includes as many practices as possible which, taken together, highlight the key elements of the attacking football that has earned West Ham United a glowing reputation all over the world.

Having spent most of his working life at West Ham, Tony is a 'Hammer' through and through. He continues to do great things with the club's youth system, coaching youngsters in the unique 'West Ham Way'. This book has benefited hugely from his insight and experience as a full-time coach and is written from his unique perspective. We both hope it will make a real difference to how football is played around the world.

Stuart Prossor

The main priority of my job as West Ham United's Youth Team coach and director of the Centre of Excellence is to produce a steady supply of players for the West Ham First Team. Every year, the continuous cycle begins with a new group of nine- to ten-year-old boys who, if well coached, may one day play for West Ham.

This book has been written with youth coaches in mind, but virtually every practice can be used with senior players, up to and including internationals – all you need to recognize is that at youth level the coaching points are directed more at the individual, while with senior players coaching focuses on specific areas, such as the midfield or defence, and the emphasis is on team organization. In addition, women's soccer is growing rapidly in both numbers and status – many professional clubs have girls' and women's teams playing in their own leagues – and the practices, drills and games provided in this book are just as relevant to girls as they are to boys, although for simplicity's sake I have referred to players as 'he' throughout.

Any practice is only as good as the coach employing it. Learning to coach well comes through experience, watching and listening, and, of course, trial and error. It takes time – this book will not make you a good coach overnight. However, combined with your own knowledge and enthusiasm, it should help you to see coaching in a different light and to understand that it is the *simple* practices, not the complicated ones, that are important. At all times, coaches should be adding to their players' natural game and promoting the straightforward principles that will begin to make the players move and pass more intelligently.

I joined West Ham United at the age of 15, straight from school and just after England had won the World Cup. I turned professional two years later, in 1968, and spent three years at West Ham as a professional before my playing career was curtailed by a broken leg. In 1973, I received a phone call from John Lyall, asking me to start coaching as part of the West Ham schoolboy system. Seven years later, I became the full-time Youth Team manager, and since then I have also had a four-year spell with the Reserves, served as director of the club's Centre of Excellence and worked alongside Billy Bonds for a year with the senior players. When Harry Redknapp became assistant manager (and now manager), I reverted to Youth Team manager and took overall responsibility for the West Ham youth set-up.

Tony Carr and members of the West Ham United Youth Squad share a joke during a break in training.

The first manager I worked for was Ron Greenwood, but John Lyall was the biggest influence on my career, and the West Ham footballing tradition that has always been a part of me was absorbed mostly while watching and working with John. Since his departure in 1989, I have shared it with Lou Macari, Billy Bonds and Harry Redknapp, who have all maintained the club's philosophy of playing entertaining football. Over time, I have developed some of my own coaching ideas to add to the great football education I was given by John and West Ham, but I have never sacrificed the principles of playing the 'West Ham Way'.

Coaches come from all over the world to visit West Ham United's training ground at Chadwell Heath, but no matter where they come from they have one thing in common – they all want coaching ideas. They already understand the principles of the game and know how they want to play, but they all ask, 'How do I teach my kids to pass the ball? How do I develop 'pass and move'? How do I get my players to produce quality football? What training routines do you use? What are your ideas?' I usually organize some practice sessions to help them find the answers to these questions, but in the end there are so many practices that I use at West Ham to develop players that the only way to help coaches worldwide was to put my ideas together in this book.

Tony Carr

WHAT COACHING IS ABOUT

Good football coaching

As a youth coach, my programme of work focuses on refining players' technique. My job is to teach all the game's basic skills, from control and passing to tackling and heading; when working with older players, the programme becomes more orientated towards team play and the need for organization. I always give the players in my care a good grounding in basic technique when they are young, because it is only by doing this that they will end up properly prepared for senior football. The players I produce will be good all-round, creative players, well equipped for the team's requirements.

Football is essentially a simple game based on intelligent interpassing. For young players, skills, technique and good movement are most easily grasped in a simple form. Consequently, in preparing players for the senior game, many of the drills I use do not involve defences and opponents. I only gradually add opposition to the drills, so that players can learn to play what is termed a 'one- and two-touch passing game' *before* confronting the difficulties of dealing with the opposition. By coaching players in this way, I prepare them for the time when they will face opponents and endeavour to hang on to possession. Nowadays, possession of the ball is the number one priority in the game, and the desire and skill needed to keep possession should be paramount, because good-quality passing then means that players can create and exploit space in the final third of the pitch.

This book will show you how the Youth Team and the Youth Section operate by describing the practices used to develop the young players at West Ham United. Of course, there is an abundance of additional practices I could have included, all of which can play a part in developing players, but space did not permit. However, I feel that those I have included are the most important and should help to stimulate any coach's imagination, so that you can both enhance these practices and add some of your own style in order to achieve your objectives.

All the drills described are stage-managed, but they are based on situations that can be expected to occur regularly in real games. In play, it is always up to the players to look, think and make the correct decisions while attempting to play top-quality, attacking football. These drills will help you to prepare players for this challenge.

Coaching is hard work, and your efforts will only be as good as the preparation you put in beforehand. Plan your sessions to progress from stage to stage, but also be flexible enough to digress during practice when problems arise that can be sorted out then and there.

Try to train in groups, with the aim of instilling basic principles such as 'play the way you are facing, keep it simple, and leave balls playable' in order to develop good habits, which over a period of time will become part of your players' natural game.

Fault diagnosis

Diagnosing faults is a fundamental part of a coach's job. You will need to watch practice sessions carefully to see what is going wrong, isolate where the faults lie, explain your diagnosis to the players and then coach against the problem recurring.

For example, consider why a move breaks down: is it the delivery of the passing player, or the control of the receiving player? Is there

Rio Ferdinand is the latest youth product from West Ham to make an impact on the game. Originally a midfield player, he has developed into an outstanding central defender.

a lack of movement? Is the coaching area too small? Is the practice too advanced for the players? If a cross comes into the box and a player goes to head the ball but misses the goal completely, the coach must consider the reasons: was it the player's approach to the ball that was at fault? Was it his body position at the point when he made contact? Did he turn his head as he went up for the header? Did he keep his eyes on the ball?

I am critical of coaches who set up practices but then do not correct faults. They make general statements such as, 'That wasn't very good' or 'That was poor', which merely state the obvious but help no one. What a coach needs to do is identify exactly where the problem lies, and then help to correct the fault. Too many coaches see a practice and copy it, without realizing that it will be only as effective as their ability actually to *coach*. A coach who knows how to diagnose – and correct – faults can develop the simplest practice into a very technical session.

Nevertheless, coaching has to be about meaningful practices if you want to improve the quality of your players and win games. The key is to study your team over two or three weeks. Take one aspect of their game at a time and analyse it, look at the individuals and the groups of players involved, think things through rationally and then ask yourself how you can correct faults through practice. Then, with specific weaknesses in mind, prepare your sessions.

Coaching technical skills

As a coach, you will need to nurture your players' technical ability, as well as improving general play such as passing and moving. Technical work is something no player should neglect at any stage of his career, whether he is a schoolboy or an international.

To be a good coach, you will need to judge when to push a player and present challenges that will stretch him but not push him beyond his capabilities; in general, the more gifted the player, the more he should be challenged. It is up to the coach to assess individuals, pushing the players who have the capacity to understand the work and perform the particular skills.

The technical work presented in this book may often seem over simple, but that is the magic of many of these drills. As a coach, you should never lose sight of the fact that the game itself is simple. In my opinion, a great coach is one who has the expertise to break down the game's technical requirements into an understandable form and develop drills to refine these basic skills.

Unopposed play

Unopposed play, as used in this book, is ideally conducted with as much match pace as your players can generate. The speed of a match is constantly changing – slow, quick, hold up, pass – and the drills should reflect this. I make no apologies for teaching technique and movement using unopposed practices: the West Ham Youth Section's priority is to develop good basic habits, and it is easier for young players to perfect these when there is no pressure from defenders.

Passing and moving

The word 'movement' is something that visitors will hear regularly at any professional training ground, but it is really just a fancy name for 'running'. All the great players know when to time their runs and where to run: running for the sake of it and flying about all over the pitch is a trait of poor players who let their hearts rule their heads. Running has to be *intelligent* – this can be coached – and must be based on the philosophy of 'pass and move'.

Passing and moving shifts defenders, and whenever a player receives the ball he should already be assessing the situation: 'Can I put the ball in there? Can I play it forward? Can I play it over the top? Should I play it to feet? Should I run with it?' The coach's job is to help prepare players for making these decisions and to teach them to create options for each other by making intelligent runs.

Paul Ince, always a great competitor, is one of the world's best midfield players.

PRACTICE DRILLS IN THIS BOOK

The practice drills are presented in this book under seven headings: technique; attacking play; 'third man' running; setting up play; wall passing; crossing; and defending. Each drill is accompanied by a diagram and/or photograph, and a key to the annotations used in the diagrams is given below.

Key to diagrams

RW right-winger
LW left-winger
RB right-back
LB left-back
OR outside-right
OL outside-left
MID midfielder
player's run
pass
run with the ball (dribble)

Many of the drills make use of 10-yard square grids, either singly or 'stacked up' in various arrangements to mark out the required area. At West Ham, we have these grids marked out with white-painted lines, but coaches without this facility can use discs or cones to divide up their pitch in the same way.

Where drills are shown as taking place on one side of the pitch or grid area, with players moving in one direction or using one foot or side of their body, these should *always* be practised in 'mirror image' as well.

Technique

The drills and training routines in this book begin by looking at ways in which a coach can best improve the technique of young players. It is a natural starting point: good technique is *essential* if young players are to fulfil their potential, and especially so if they want to play a pass-and-move game. This book presents drills that will assist the players you coach to develop their ability to manipulate the ball and keep possession. These drills can be staged both outdoors and, when the weather is bad, in the gym.

As an example of the use of these skills, imagine that a ball is drilled at the receiver and he decides to pass or lay it off to a team-mate – he will need to take the pace off the ball in order to leave it playable for his colleague and maintain the pass-and-move rhythm of the game. To do this, he needs good technique and good ball skills. A great exponent of the technique needed to lay off the ball and maintain a quick tempo of play is Eric Cantona. He can leave the ball stone dead for team-mates, putting just the correct pace on it for the receiver, or drop it into space for a runner off the ball.

Technically, the Brazilians are one of the most gifted footballing nations, with every

Control on the instep. Showing good control, the player uses his arms and body to protect the ball as he makes contact. Using the inside of his foot, he relaxes the surface on contact to take any pace off the ball. From this position, he can also pass the ball first time to supporting players.

generation – from Pele right through to Romario and Juninho today – producing some superb players. In particular, the Brazilians appreciate the value of getting their bodies into good positions to receive the ball, so that they can proceed swiftly to the next movement or pass. Technically, they are light years ahead of us, and are quite brilliant at receiving the ball from any direction, and then turning in any direction without losing control of it. Their great flexibility and all-round movement, coupled with excellent technique, means that the pass-and-move tempo of the Brazilian game is very high.

When space is at a premium in the last third of the pitch, good technique is essential, otherwise possession will be lost. This is where the Brazilians really come into their own. They position themselves between the defender and the ball, and are strong in the upper body and beautifully balanced on their feet. They immediately get in line with the approaching ball and use their great first touch to retain possession. In this area of the pitch, good technique is needed in order to

Juninho displays upper body strength and good balance while keeping possession of the ball.

Control on the thigh. As the ball falls on to his bent leg, the player drops his knee away to relax the thigh and thereby gain instant control, at the same time making sure that he keeps his body between ball and defender.

manufacture a scoring chance: the Brazilians usually have it in abundance.

A player's technique is tested fully when an opponent applies pressure as the ball is received. The player must be relaxed so that his body can act like a cushion, for if the ball meets a rigid foot, thigh or chest it will bounce off and possession is usually forfeited. You will often hear coaches on the sidelines shouting at players to 'pressure the first touch' – the first touch is the key to becoming a quality player, and if a player has a problem controlling the ball he will have problems *full stop*. Try to pressure the first touch of Juventus players and you will not get near the ball, because their technique is good enough for them to play under pressure. Their coaches know that you cannot play football in a pass-and-move style if the team's technique is poor.

Preparing to receive the ball on the half-turn.

Turning with the ball is an added discipline. This book will help you coach players in receiving the ball in the 'half-turn position'. This allows the player to lay the ball back, to roll on the outside of the defender having controlled the ball, or to roll on the inside by letting the ball run. John Lyall – and Ron Greenwood before him – always emphasized that this gives the players so many more options. The technique drills will help to develop players who always stand 'half-turned' and will teach them the vital importance of adjusting their feet when receiving the ball.

Shooting is the most exciting aspect of the game and, once again, technique is the key. The 'full-instep volley' is the most spectacular goal-scoring technique: on the British scene, this has been the trademark of Welsh international striker Mark Hughes (Manchester United, Barcelona and Chelsea) and the England manager Glenn Hoddle when he played for Tottenham Hotspur and England. Newcastle United's former manager Kevin Keegan was another brilliant practitioner of this volley, as was Bryan 'Pop' Robson, a 'Hammer' during two stints in the 1970s. The drills in this book will help you to perfect your players' shooting and volleying.

Good technique will also allow the naturally gifted dribblers to develop their skills and exploit their balance. West Ham have always had their fair share of technically 'clever' players like Trevor Brooking, Alan Devonshire and, more recently, Paulo Futre. They have helped to reinforce the idea that

Glenn Hoddle – an excellent volleyer of the ball, showing this in spectacular fashion.

space is created when an individual player can take an opponent out of the game with a dribbling skill, which is possible only if the player has the grounding in technique that this book will help you develop.

Attacking Play

With a solid grounding in technique established, you can now begin to coach your players in attacking play. At West Ham, we try to get the ball into the final third of the pitch, around the penalty box or behind the opposition's defence using good passing and movement. The greater the control we achieve in the last third, the greater the likelihood that we can dictate the terms of the game to our opponents. The 'attacking' drills and movements we practise to prepare for matches will also help you to prepare your players for the time when they will face similar situations in games.

This style of coaching educates young players to probe and penetrate the opposition with as much accuracy as possible in the final third of the pitch. With this in mind, many of the practices are based on quick interpassing to link an attacking player with his back to goal – who can play the way he is facing – to his team-mates, who are looking for space around and behind him.

The drills aim to teach young players never to give away possession. I tell them constantly: 'Don't throw the ball in there. Don't give it away. Keep possession, and only put it in there if you are sure you have a runner or target to pick out.' I am also aiming to establish patience in the mind of the players.

The West Ham attacking strategy starts with the goalkeeper, who tries to feed defenders with the ball in order to start an attack. Defenders are encouraged to bring the ball out of defence, and this book will help you to drill players in the skills this requires. The Germans appreciate better than anyone that attack begins in defence – the brilliant central defender Matthias Sammer helped them to win the Euro '96 championship by making and scoring excellent goals. In fact, all the better European footballing nations, as well as the South Americans, have known for years that this is the way to play football. British coaches are at last beginning to realize that if their teams can break out from the back, retaining control of the ball, and

Matthias Sammer demonstrates the art of breaking out of defence with the ball, which he did with great style during Euro '96.

'join' the midfield, they stand a far better chance of keeping possession in order to produce a telling, measured pass which can punish the opposition in the crucial final third.

Some of the drills in this book involve players learning to attack from defence in threes. In the late 1970s and early 1980s, some of the best football West Ham United played involved the trio comprised of midfielders Trevor Brooking and Alan Devonshire, and full-back Frank Lampard, who provided the link between defence and attack. A little earlier, in the 1960s and 1970s, West Ham's captain, Bobby Moore, and Germany's Franz Beckenbauer were masters at breaking out from the back. In the modern

Ruud Gullit is an exceptionally talented midfield player who has also played the role of a central defender, breaking forward into attacking positions.

era, the tremendously talented Ruud Gullit has also filled this type of role. Coach a player who is comfortable attacking with the ball from the back and you will develop a player who is able to play in this style.

The drills are also designed to encourage passing and moving in the final third of the pitch, with a view to engineering a strike at goal. Late runs from midfield are an important part of this. In the modern game, David Platt of Arsenal and England has been a great exponent of this tactic. His understanding of space and timing is first class, and his goal-scoring record for England in this role is exceptional. In the 1960s, Martin Peters (West Ham and England) had a similar grasp of the importance of moving into space – an understanding of 'leaving the space unoccupied as late as possible' before finally making a run, arriving just as the ball does.

However, passing angles are perhaps the key to good attacking play. I have always been critical of players who run, look and pass in straight lines. This vision of the game is very narrow and results in wide players simply putting the ball down the line. Instead, they should be thinking along the lines of, 'What is on the angle to the left? Can I change the direction of play?'

At senior level, many clubs play one-dimensional football: the long ball game. To some extent, this is the result of managers being under pressure to win matches and is therefore completely understandable. It will not, however, produce creative players. The 'West Ham Way' is to pass short *and* long and to play angles, not just straight lines. Teams which believe that the more they get the ball behind the other team, the more chance they have of scoring will more often than not concede possession. Equally, things break down if the players off the ball stand still or fail to make the correct runs and passing angles for the player in possession. The great Dutch coach Wiel Coerver once said, 'Before anyone can play football, they have to learn to play the short passing game. If you have a short passing game you can play any system.' Coaching at youth level is not about winning, but development.

'Third Man' Running

Another aspect of successful attacking play is 'third man' running. Football is not a game that involves only the player on the ball and one player off it. When the ball is played to a target man, there should be someone else off the play who runs to support the receiver. The passer is thus released from his job of immediately supporting the target man in front of him and should recognize that he can now make a 'third man' forward run. In fact, all that these three players are doing is making the best use of the space available.

At West Ham, we have always put great emphasis on 'third man' running. Obviously we did not invent it, but we do try to develop the skill more thoroughly than some other clubs. It is no good being technically a good passer of the ball if all you do is stand still afterwards and admire your pass. During the 1960s and 1970s at the club, Bobby Moore would look up from the back and pick out Johnny Byrne or Geoff Hurst, West Ham's target men. They had good enough technique to receive the ball on their chest or thighs, and to set it back with one touch to Ronnie Boyce, Martin Peters or Trevor Brooking, who all had the skill to spot the 'third man' runner and deliver the pass.

In teaching players 'third man' running on the training ground, I always demand that they pay attention to making wide angles. I regularly tell the players: 'Keep making wide angles and more room will become available for you to use.' What movement does is create space, and the more space that is created, the more time the man on the ball will have to make his pass or take his shot.

The art of 'third man' running lies in the speed of execution. In some respects, 'third man' running has become more difficult in recent years, because although there is more space behind defenders, the space in front has been squeezed and condensed. Consequently, I go to extra lengths to emphasize the 'third man' running principles to young players. This is because in the heat of battle, the thought process must be very quick. I make them repeat exercises and movements over and over again, so that it all becomes second nature, and when thinking time is at a premium in a competitive match

As the ball is being set back, the support player makes a wide angle to receive the pass.

the run or pass will be instinctive. The longer it takes to deliver the pass to the 'third man' runner, the greater the likelihood that the ball will be cut out or picked off, or that the runner may be offside or marked by a faster-thinking defender.

Forwards with the ability to lay off the ball with just one touch are a great asset in developing good 'third man' running play. Ideally, you should try to develop in your players the skill of setting the ball back with one touch and leaving it playable for the receiver, thus giving him more time to make his decisions.

According to Ron Greenwood and John Lyall, the way to receive the ball was by 'coming off on the half-turn and using the back foot'. This book contains the drills that should help to develop this in your players. Watching the best European footballers confirmed to me the importance of the position of a player's body and feet when receiving the ball. You should be aiming to instil in your young players the skill of receiving the ball 'on the back foot', with body half-turned or sideways on. Good technique is important in this, too.

In the early 1960s, two of West Ham's finest players, John 'Budgie' Byrne and Geoff Hurst, were great models of forward play. Byrne, who buzzed around, could knock a ball off one-touch, left or right foot, on the volley, and set the ball back, instigating movement for players like Martin Peters to be on the end of a 'third man' run. He was a great technician. Alongside him was Geoff Hurst, the perfect target and a man of physical stature, who would stand and face the man on the ball. He was good in the air, held balls up and could get on the end of through balls. Using the drills in this book, you will be able to coach players to exploit any similar talent and to develop the ability to make 'third man' runs.

Setting Up Play

It is not only target men who must be capable of setting up attacking play. Any player can find himself in a position where he will be expected to receive the ball and initiate an attacking move, either by laying off the ball and developing a move incorporating 'third man' running, or by turning with the ball himself.

Setting a ball back on the half-turn, which should trigger forward movement.

Setting up play is a constant theme in all our work at West Ham. In the modern game defences are highly organized and you must be confident enough to 'play in to marked players' and move opposing defenders around to break down the defence as a whole. The drills in this book will help you to develop in your players the ability to receive the ball with their back to goal and play the way they are facing, and to open up defences by movement, making space for penetrating passes.

Setting up play involves two disciplines: first, the delivery of the ball to the front men; and, second, the way in which the front men decide to hold the ball, control it, turn, or deliver the next pass. Paul Goddard, of the 1980–1 West Ham promotion side, was a master at receiving the ball when marked. He could turn defenders and just as readily lay off the ball, one-touch, to supporting players. He provided the 'springboard' for most of the attacking movement, and knowing that nine out of ten balls would be laid back or held up created options for good forward passing and movement. Paul learnt his skills through constant practice in playing with his back to goal, and this book contains the most important of the drills used to perfect his art.

Liverpool led the way between the early 1970s and the end of the 1980s with fast, interchanging one- and two-touch passing movements. Routines similar to the ones they developed – with a high skill level and completed at speed – can move defenders around so that space appears for goal-scoring opportunities. At West Ham, Trevor Brooking and Alan Devonshire both revelled in receiving passes while being marked, because they were confident in their own ability to play the ball with one touch and then move again, to hold it if necessary and beat their marker, or to draw him out of a defending situation and use the space behind.

The drills and routines in this book are designed to help your players develop the skills needed to set up attacking plays.

Wall Passing

The 'wall pass', or 'one-two', is a ploy that is as old as football, and is one of the most effective pass-and-move disciplines you can develop in young players. Consequently, it is worth spending plenty of time practising this simple skill. If the wall pass can be exploited efficiently, it is an effective tactic for getting behind 'compact' modern defences or through 'tight' midfields.

At the top level of the game, there are technically gifted players in all areas, and most also possess pace. If done quickly and precisely – in the way that the Italians demonstrate week in, week out – the wall pass is a simple way of breaking down even the most talented defence. Practice will reap handsome rewards: Paul Ince was a great exponent of this move when playing for the West Ham Youth Team in the mid-1980s. His passing at speed, combined with his pace and strength, made him a real threat to any defence we played.

Crossing

Practising crosses on the training ground can produce results at the highest levels of the game. The drills in this book will help your players to develop skills – such as the cross to the near post – which have played a major part in winning the game's greatest honours.

The near-post cross was introduced at West Ham United in the early 1960s by Ron Greenwood, who went on to manage England. He was a very inventive coach who brought a lot of Continental training methods to the club. During our very successful 1960s period (1964 FA Cup Winners, 1965 European Cup Winners' Cup Winners and a strong representation in the 1966 England World Cup-winning side), Ron coached us to exploit space at the near post with accurate crosses. He told the First Team strikers, Geoff Hurst and Johnny Byrne, to make runs into this area and the rest of the team was then instructed to feed this space. Accuracy was, of course, crucial, so Ron made all the players – and especially the wide players, Peter Brabrook and John Sissons – practise putting the ball into this space. I can remember spending hours as a young apprentice driving, chipping, bending and crossing balls around wooden posts (representing defenders) into this near-post area.

The benefits came in spectacular fashion during the World Cup Finals in 1966. Most of us recall (or will have seen highlights of) the quarter-final in which England played Argentina, and the way in which the stalemate

Geoff Hurst in a classic striker's pose as he prepares to shoot: head down, eyes on the ball and good balance.

was broken by Geoff Hurst's match-winning goal. It came from a tactic practised on the West Ham training ground: Martin Peters, in a wide left position deep in the Argentina half, curled the ball left-footed into the area on the near post and Geoff Hurst attacked the space, heading to score. In the Final itself against the Germans, the near-post cross worked again. The great Bobby Moore placed the ball for a free kick on the German right and chipped the ball into space, for Geoff Hurst to score. We all know the rest!

Perfect crossing is not always rewarded with a World Cup, but the drills in this book should help your players to develop their crossing ability and win many matches, whatever their level.

Defending

The final set of drills in this book is aimed at helping you to coach players to defend. Predominantly, at West Ham, we defend 'zonally', with either three or four defenders patrolling particular areas or 'zones'. On odd occasions and in certain situations we mark an outstanding individual man-to-man, but I find this a very rigid system and in some respects it restricts your own creative endeavours, although I would advocate it when defending set plays such as corners and free kicks.

At West Ham, we started experimenting with a 'flat back three' – a zonal system operating with three central defenders marking two central strikers – during our successful 1995–6 Youth Team campaign. Two of the three defenders are predominantly 'markers', and the 'spare player' – the *libero* – will pick up and mark the strikers as they move around. This differs from the old Italian *catenaccio* system – strict man-to-man marking with a deeper sweeper who is always a free man – as the 'flat back three' do not have players that they have to follow everywhere and always mark.

The late Bobby Moore showing the style and control that characterized his game.

In this innovative defence system, the right and left full-backs mark whoever comes into their area and are also free to forage forward, having been released from the majority of covering responsibilities. The extra central defender means that the full-backs effectively become 'wing-backs' who are free to push right up, although this may leave them vulnerable to the ball over the top into space behind them. However, one of the three central defenders should be comfortable 'picking off' any balls that are pushed into areas behind the wing-backs.

The key, however, is to have the technique to play any system and to understand what good defending entails. The drills in this book should enable you to equip your players to adapt to any system and to defend as a unit.

ASSESSING YOUNG PLAYERS

Any coach is delighted to find a talented player – but how do you judge who is or isn't talented, and how do you balance first impressions with long-term prospects? You can assess the merits of young players using six criteria:

1 Natural ability and technique/skill.
2 Knowledge and awareness.
3 Courage and bravery.
4 Character and mental toughness.
5 Speed and mobility.
6 Anticipation.

Spotting an outstanding player may seem easy, and it is true that talent is very obvious, but in the early schoolboy years young players are unlikely to be blessed with all six distinctions. I choose players for the West Ham United youth programme who are gifted in as many as possible of the six classifications.

Judging young players can be tricky. It is easy to form a favourable first impression and invite a boy to the club, but after a number of weeks he may not turn out to be the player we thought he was. By the same token, a player we thought was borderline can turn out to be better than expected. At least, though, within the club environment we can see what he does 'naturally' and will have a chance to assess whether or not he has good technical ability. When he plays in small-sided games, we will find out whether he sees other players and is aware of what is going on around him, and, later, whether he transfers this ability into effective 11- against-11 play.

Some young boys have a 'natural gift'. They 'make things happen', and make other people play. They demand that other boys 'Give it here, give it back.' This tells me that these individuals have a more advanced understanding and knowledge of the game than others in their age group.

In my work, I constantly use the phrase, 'Lively minds, lively bodies' to reinforce the fact that a young player must at all times be alert, ready for any eventuality, and seeking to be one step ahead of the opposition. Courage and bravery is also important. This will become evident in situations where a defender or forward may have to put himself at risk in being first to the ball, either to score or to make a last-ditch interception.

Later, as the players get older, the coach will have to develop collective elements such as team spirit, the will to win, competitiveness, urgency, aggression and 'mental toughness'. Players should be encouraged to show that they can stand up for themselves while remaining disciplined enough to play in a team's pattern.

A young player's technical ability may not be as polished as his coach would like it to be. However, if he possesses mobility, athleticism and is also very quick it may be possible to improve his skills to complement these natural gifts. The attribute of 'pace' is very important in the modern game; 'mobility' is another crucial factor. Ask yourself: 'Does this player move well? Is he quick?' If the answer to both is yes, then the task facing you is to enhance these natural gifts with footballing technique and skills which can be instilled on the training ground.

However, although physical speed is very important, 'speed of thought' – the ability to play quickly and early, and to read situations – can make up for a lack of real pace. This quality can be instilled in players by using situations in training which make them more prepared for and able to anticipate situations before they develop. When I am talking to young players I often say: 'Your brain makes you react to situations, and if you see things quickly your body will react accordingly.'

The great England captain Bobby Moore, for example, was not the quickest of players, but he was a wonderful reader of the game, with great anticipation. As a 15-year-old at West Ham United many years ago, I remember our manager Ron Greenwood asking after a coaching session: 'What do you think I look for in a young player ? What is the one essential ingredient?' Everybody came up with the usual answers – pace, skill and so on – but he answered with one word: anticipation. Ask yourself: 'Does this young player go to the ball? Does he see the cross coming? Is he making runs off the ball? Does he *anticipate*? Anticipation is a natural, not an acquired attribute. All the world's great players today have – and those in the past had – this quality, a knack of sensing what is going to happen and, accordingly, knowing where to be when. A coach needs to analyse this gift, asking himself: 'What is it? And how can I recognize it in young players?'

PREPARING TO PLAY

The skills that your players should pick up by practising the drills in this book are those they will need in order to play the game successfully. But once they are equipped with a good technique and knowledge of the game, in order to maximize the amount of football they enjoy you must also take care of them physically. Nobody should go into match play, or even a practice session, where they will be expected to perform all the degrees of movement that football requires, without first warming up their body and stretching their muscles.

Warming up for practice

As a general rule, to get players ready to go into training at a fair pace, I begin with a gentle ten-minute jog. Then we stretch for the next five minutes, completing a range of different exercises. Starting with the neck muscles, we exercise the shoulder muscles, the trunk and waist area, then twist and turn the body, stretch the groin and the top half of the legs, work down the calves to the Achilles tendons, and then finish with the ankle joints. We then repeat the jogging, introducing jumping and turning, before doing some light ball work during which everybody tries to avoid contact. I slowly speed up the tempo which ups the players' pulse rate, and after five to ten minutes we have a good stretch again. With young players the warm-up should take approximately 15–20 minutes in total.

Once the players are fully warmed up, you can begin training. At first, it may seem a long way off, but each simple drill and practice is preparing the players for the time in the future when they will play 11-a-side at a level that will test their abilities to the full.

Preparing for a match

When it comes to a match, the coach should know how he wants his team to play and the basic tactical system/formation he will employ. The manager or coach should have nurtured the team's playing style during the training sessions and have given the players a clear understanding of the tactical shape he expects them to adopt. It does not matter what the playing style happens to be: if, during the game, the players fall below the standards the coach has set them, or they do not adhere to the framework, he may remind them from the touchline of the lessons learned on the training ground!

Tactical approach

When the players go out on the football field, collectively they should know what you want them to do. At West Ham, we work all week on passing and moving, and in the dressing room before a match I remind the boys: 'Pass the ball well and pass it quickly!'

Of course, the coach might believe in a 'playing' philosophy, but, with the game becoming so much more result-orientated in senior football all over the world, sometimes at this level the coach may have to compromise his principles, because the players at his disposal are not technically capable of playing in a certain way. At youth level, where results are not so crucial, the coach can have far more influence on how the players approach their matches.

Mental approach

At youth and schoolboy level, however, the result is not all-important. It is natural to be annoyed by poor results, but I do not mind youngsters making mistakes. As long as they are trying to do the right things, I can live with a few errors.

Above all, when dealing with young players you must set high standards and demand that the players meet them. If you do, there will be times ahead when you will feel proud of what they have achieved – when something you have worked hard at on the training ground produces dividends on the pitch.

32 9988
DAGENHAM MOTORS

1 TECHNIQUE

THE JOB OF coaching young players begins with developing their technique so that they can control, pass and move, eventually all in one movement. The further a player goes in the game, the tighter his control of the ball has to be. The final objective is for the player to be able to control the ball in one movement, take the ball in his stride, cushion a pass and guide the ball to his teammates.

If the ball is driven at the player, he needs to be able to take the pace off it. If the ball is coming slowly, he needs to be able to put pace on it. He needs to leave the ball playable for his teammates. Overall, he needs to develop a 'feel' for the ball. Technique can be improved dramatically through continued practice and should always be worked on, no matter what the age and experience of the player or the level at which he is playing.

PASS AND MOVE

The drills in this section are designed to improve a player's basic technique and ability to pass and move by making him perform in a confined space in preparation for the full 11-a-side game.

Piggy-in-the-middle

The 'piggy-in-the-middle' drill (Figure 1) is well known to coaches. A small group of up to eight players can improve their technique by playing it. In the basic drill, the ball is passed from player to player and the 'piggy' has to try to win it or force it out of the area of play.

Variations for advanced players include using a circle within a 10-yard square grid – if the ball goes outside its circumference, the piggy changes. This denies players the option of backing away and making the circle bigger, which would give them more time and space. You can also add a second piggy, let players use only the right or left foot, allow only two touches, and invite challenges from the piggy in order to help develop quick feet. In addition, you can ban the receiver from passing back to the player who gave him the ball.

If the group is larger than eight, the players can be asked to keep the ball off the ground using volleys and headers, allowing as many touches as their technique warrants, or you can introduce extra piggies.

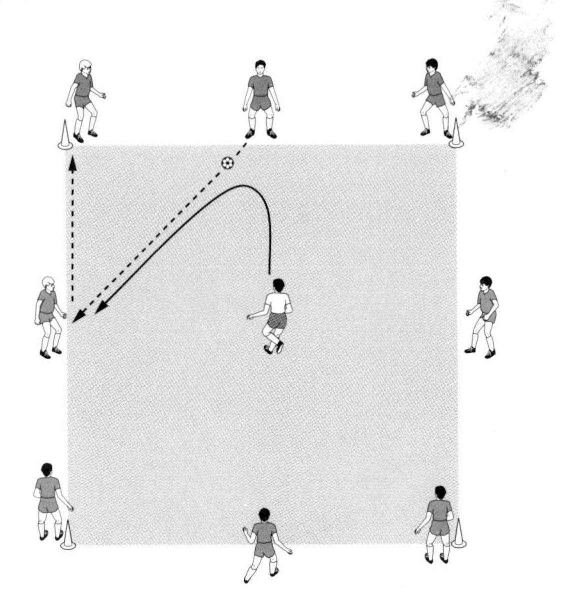

Figure 1

Push passing

Passing and moving in a confined space (Figure 2) will improve your players' passing game. Using a 10-yard square grid for the drill will keep the players quite close together, so the passing will have to be accurate.

Two players are positioned on each side of the square. Player 1 starts by push passing with his left foot to 2, who passes to 3. Player 3 passes the ball straight across to 4, who passes left to 5. After a player has completed a pass, he runs to his right. Only the top receiver, player 2, follows his own pass; he rolls the ball off to his right with his back (right) foot. Player 3 has to play off his back foot, letting the ball run across his body and stepping in to pass to 4, using his right foot. Player 4 passes left-footed to his left, to 5.

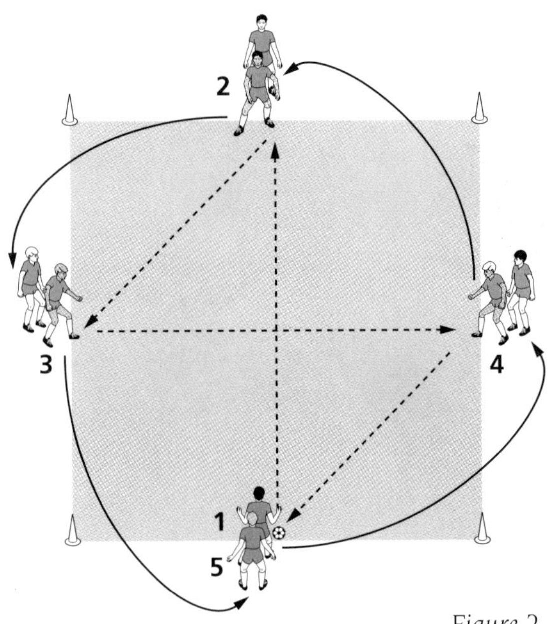

Figure 2

This drill encourages playing and the making of angles. To push pass well, the player must plant his standing foot alongside the ball, keeping his head and knee over the ball and his ankle 'tight', providing a solid surface on contact as the ball is pushed to the receiver. Players can also pass using the outside of the foot. Correct pacing of the ball is vital. Push the ball so that it is playable, preferably with one touch. It should not be pushed so hard that it is unplayable nor so slowly that it doesn't reach its target.

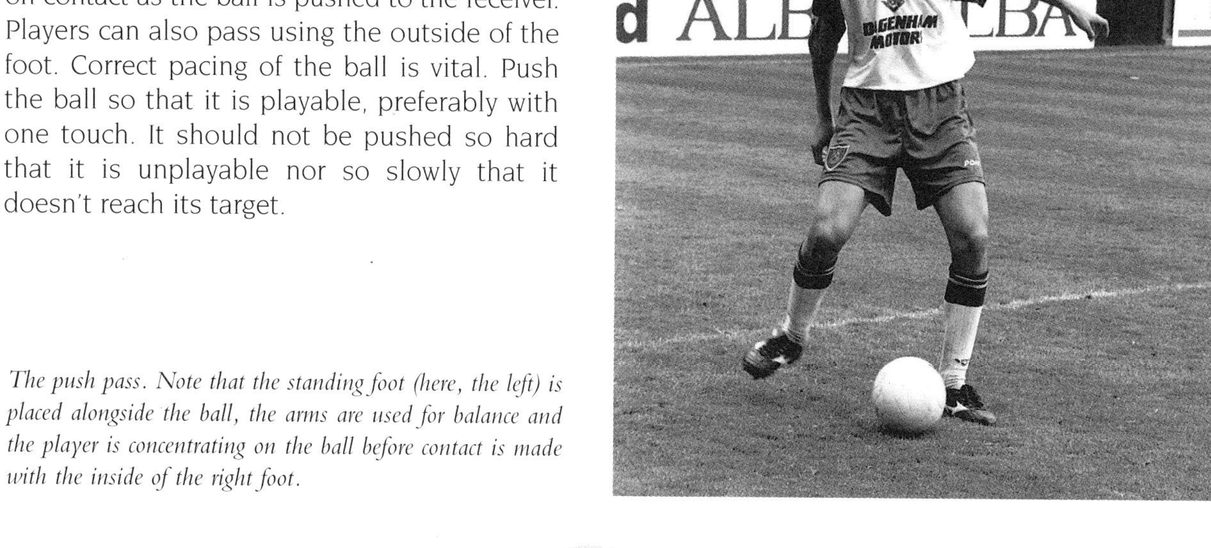

The push pass. Note that the standing foot (here, the left) is placed alongside the ball, the arms are used for balance and the player is concentrating on the ball before contact is made with the inside of the right foot.

Volleys and headers

Practising the skills of volleying and heading in a confined space will improve a player's technique. In this drill (Figure 3), three players occupy three of the corners in a 10-yard square grid, with players 1 and 3 standing in diagonally opposite corners holding a ball each. Player 2 shuttles across from corner to corner, heading one ball and volleying the other back to 1 and 3.

Player 1 serves the ball to 2, who has run from his corner and volleys the ball back. He then turns immediately to face player 3, who throws the ball for 2 to head back. Player 2 then jogs to the far corner, before turning to run and volley using his opposite foot, and to head again.

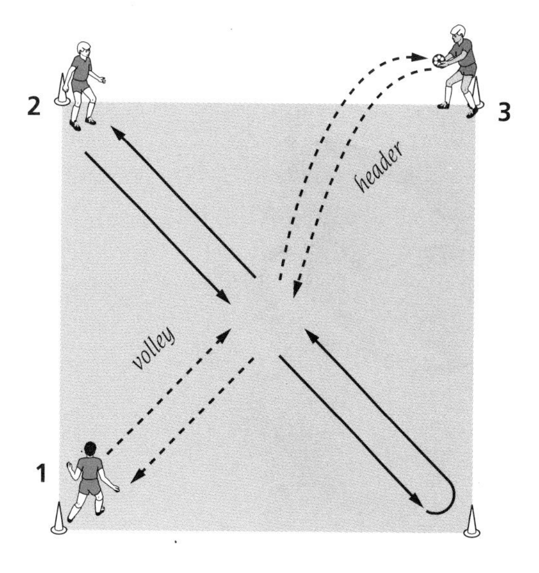

Figure 3

Back foot set-up

This drill (Figure 4) will improve a player's ability to pass on the move to a colleague on the run. Players 1 (with the ball) and 2 start in opposite corners of a 10-yard square grid. Player 2 comes to the centre of the grid and 1 lays the ball to him and then runs to the next corner. Player 2 plays the ball, on the half-turn, to the corner to which 1 is running, and then runs to the opposite corner.

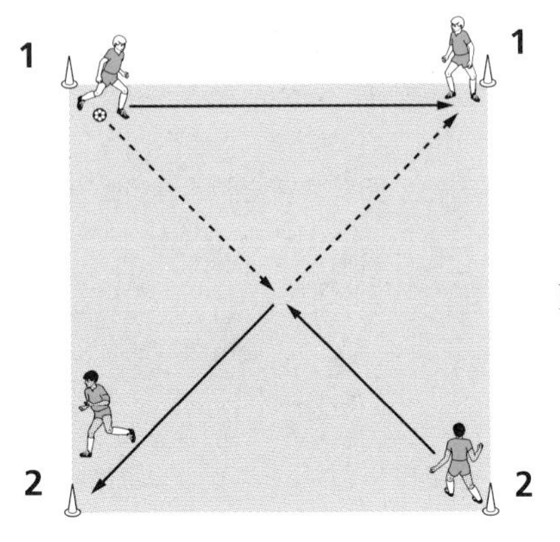

Figure 4

Wall passing

This drill (Figure 5) will teach players to move around a defender quickly and improve the technique of laying off the ball first time. Player 2 stands a little behind and to one ide of a cone in the middle of the 10-yard square grid. Player 1, the runner, dribbles towards the cone before passing to the back foot of 2, who returns it into the path of 1 on the other side of the cone.

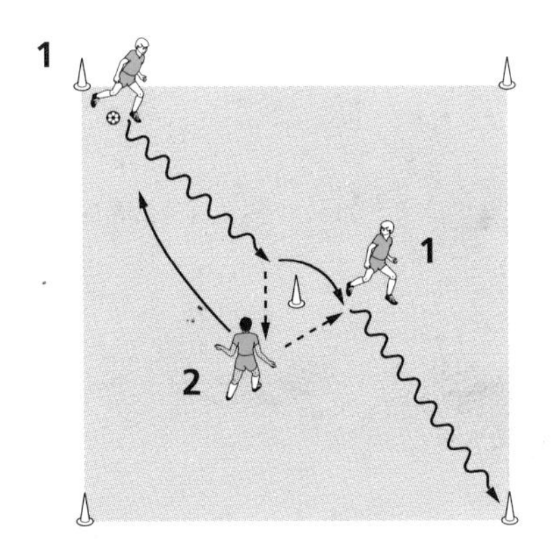

Figure 5

Turning within the circle

This drill (Figure 6) will improve players' turns in tight positions, particularly where a deep-lying striker is playing in the 'hole' behind the midfield and in front of defenders and can turn quickly to attack the opposition's defence. Player 2 stands in the middle of a 20-yard square grid or the centre circle, surrounded by players on the edge. He receives the ball from player 1 on the half-turn and performs a turning technique. Player 1 moves to the centre. After turning, player 2 passes the ball to any waiting player and runs to the outside of the circle, and the exercise is repeated.

Figure 6

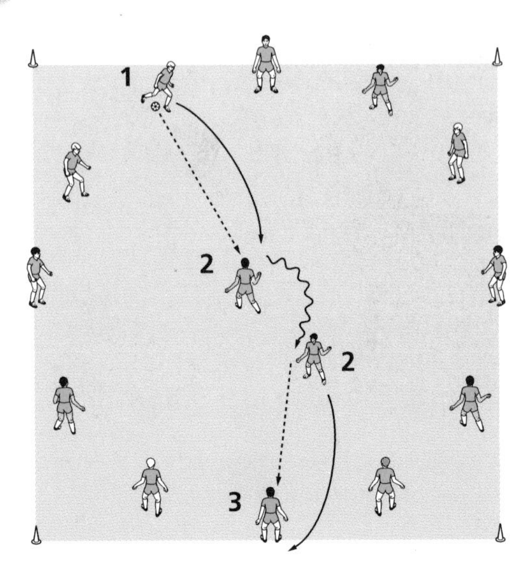

Player 3 passes to the player in the 'hole' (centre of picture), who is in the space behind the defending midfield and in front of the defenders – a position frequently taken up by deep-lying strikers such as Gianfranco Zola and Teddy Sheringham.

The receiving player is on the half-turn and controls the ball with his back foot (here, the right).

He uses a dragging action with the inside of his controlling foot (the right).

The dragging action brings the ball in front of the player as he swivels on his standing foot.

*The player has turned and is facing his opponents' goal. He can now run at the defenders (*à la *Zola) or pick out a running player with a telling pass (*à la *Sheringham).*

Wall passing across the circle

This drill (Figure 7) will improve players' ability to receive and play the ball with one touch, in wall-pass fashion. Standing on the edge of a 20-yard square grid or the centre circle, player 1 has the ball. He plays it across the circle to player 2 and then runs to make a wide receiving angle. Player 2 plays it back to 1 (who becomes the wall), before stepping into the circle and making a fresh passing angle. Player 1 returns the pass, before taking 2's place on the outside of the circle. Player 2 passes across to 3 and runs to take up his position. Player 3 links with another player to repeat the combination of passes.

The players should pass the ball quickly and leave it playable after one touch. The interchanges should be swift and runs must not be straight at the ball but directed so as to make wide angles.

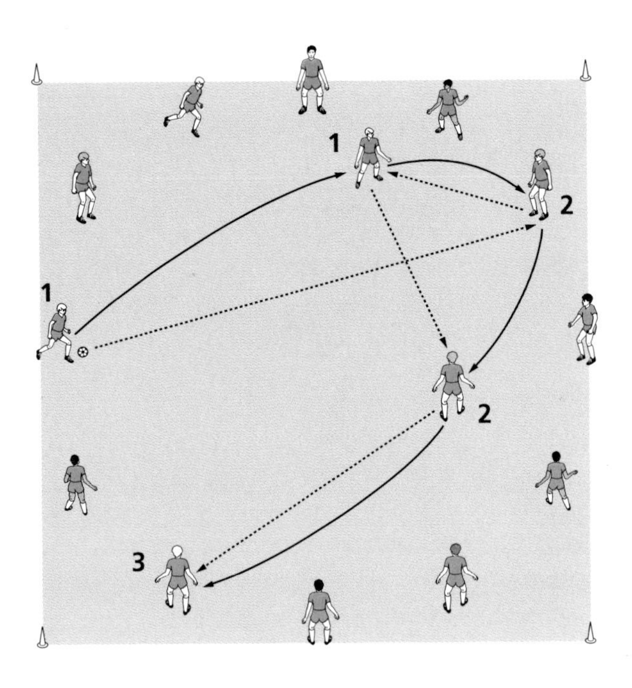

Figure 7

The spare man

Using a 10-yard square grid and two balls (Figure 8) three players (1, 2 and 3) stand apart, facing player 4, 10 yards away. The two players with balls feed them one after another to player 4, who passes to the 'spare man' who is the one currently without a ball.

This drill, which develops playing off the back foot as well as quick decision-making, can be enhanced by adding a fifth player and a third ball, or even more. You can speed up or slow down the practice as the ability of the players allows.

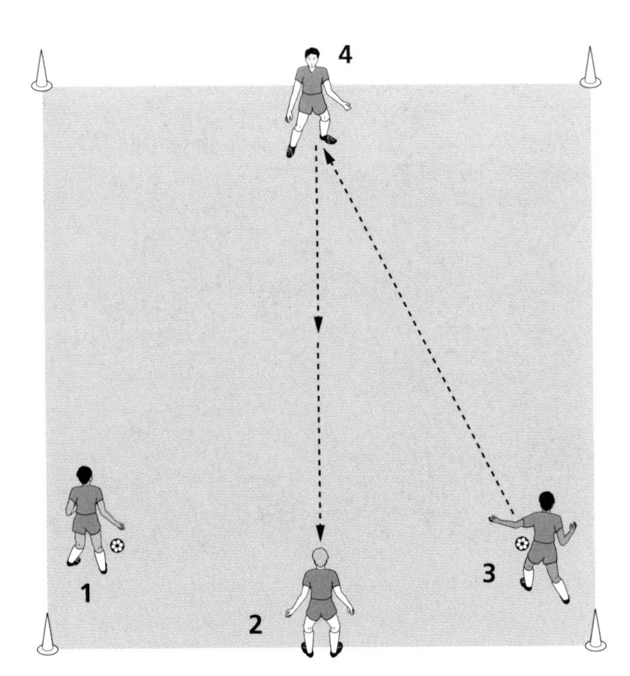

Figure 8

BALL MANIPULATION

Up to their early teenage years, children should not be restricted too greatly as it may stifle their natural dribbling abilities. But young players do have a tendency to over-run the ball, and the discipline of allowing only three touches (control, push or touch, and pass), then two touches (control and pass) and ultimately one touch (pass and move) can be useful limits to include in practice. Eventually, they must understand that space is created by passing and moving. At the highest level, it is necessary to control the ball in one movement and, in a lot of instances, pass in one movement, too. A good rule of thumb is to coach in a basic manner while trying to encourage individual skill.

The aim of the drills in this section is to familiarize young players with the feel of the ball so that they will acquire the knack of quick movement and feet adjustment. The younger the players, the more impressionable and receptive to ideas they generally are. You should coach them on a regular basis to manipulate the ball, so that when they grow up they will be more comfortable in one-against-one situations.

Ball manipulation is based on a sleight of foot followed by a quick change of direction. The player's knees should be bent and his centre of gravity low, so that he is well balanced and can transfer his body weight from left foot to right foot or vice versa. The top half of the player's body can then be moved easily, too.

Dancing and dragging

The player skips from right foot to left foot while rotating around the ball, swapping the foot on the ball and the foot on the ground as he moves in whichever direction the coach may demand: forwards, backwards, left or right. The player then drags the ball backwards or forwards using the soles of his feet.

'Dancing'. The player offers his right foot on to the ball, and then quickly releases his touch to offer his left foot in the same way. He tries to repeat the sequence quickly, mimicking a 'dancing' action. Coach the player to offer a light touch on to the ball.

Hooking the ball

The player dribbles the ball in a forward direction before wrapping the inside or the outside of his foot around it, dragging it back almost behind himself with a hooking action, and then instantly changing pace to move away.

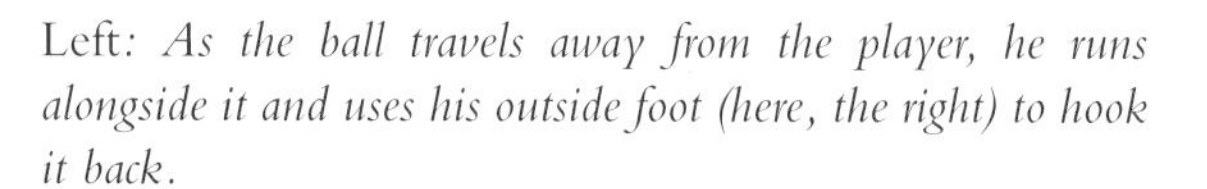

Left: *As the ball travels away from the player, he runs alongside it and uses his outside foot (here, the right) to hook it back.*

The hooking action is complete when the ball is brought back in the opposite direction to that in which it was travelling.

The player has turned and now accelerates away quickly.

Dummying over with the inside of the foot

The player dummies over the ball with the inside of, say, his right foot but uses the inside of his left foot to move the ball. Alternatively, he 'steps over' with the inside of his left foot and pushes the ball with the inside of his right. After performing the skill, he accelerates away for 5–10 yards to encourage a change of pace.

The player looks to pass the ball (here, with his right foot).

Instead of passing, he 'dummies' over the ball and plants his right foot beyond the ball. He must try to develop as much disguise as possible in order to fool the opponent.

With his weight now on his right foot, the player uses his left to push the ball away and change direction.

It is now simply a case of getting the ball out of his feet and moving away quickly.

Dummying over with the outside of the foot

The player dribbles slowly forward using the outside of, say, his right foot, before lifting the outside of this foot over the ball and planting it beyond the ball. Having dummied, he pushes the ball in the opposite direction using the outside of his left foot. The exercise is then repeated, reversing the feet. Again, after performing the skill the player accelerates away for 5–10 yards to encourage a change of pace.

Running with the ball towards a defender, the player uses sleight of foot and good balance to 'dummy', playing the ball with the outside of his foot (here, the right) and moving to the right.

Instead of playing the ball, his right foot passes over it and is planted on the ground.

With all the player's weight now on his right foot, the outside of the left foot is freed to push the ball away to the player's left.

With the dummy now complete, the player accelerates away quickly. He will need to develop good disguise and quick feet in order to perfect this technique.

Cruyff turn

Dribbling in a square, the player tucks the ball back between his legs with the inside of his foot, pushing it behind his standing leg to change direction and thus emulating the great Johan Cruyff, who excelled at this skill.

The player uses the sole of his foot (here, the right) to drag the ball back towards himself.

He performs a dragging action with the side of his foot.

Keeping contact with the ball with his right foot, the player uses his instep to manipulate the ball behind his standing leg.

With enough contact on the ball to push it behind and away from his standing leg, the player alters direction with a quick change of pace. This mimics the move perfected by the great Dutch player Johan Cruyff.

Drag back

The player puts the sole of, say, his right foot on the ball and drags it back away from an imaginary opponent, before pushing the ball with the inside of the same foot and moving away to his right as quickly as possible.

The player on the ball drags it back towards himself using the sole of his foot (here, the right).

In an instant, he releases the contact of his sole with the ball.

Using the inside of his right foot, the player changes direction by pushing the ball away at an angle to his right. Good balance and speed are the key.

Back-foot pairs

In this drill (Figure 9), two players stand in adjacent corners of a 10-yard square grid, and a third stands in the middle of the opposite side. Player 1 lays the ball up the line to 3, who moves to his right and adjusts his feet to play it across the grid with his back foot to 2, who repeats the drill down his side of the grid so that 3 can use his other foot. The players should rotate so that they can practise all three disciplines involved in this drill.

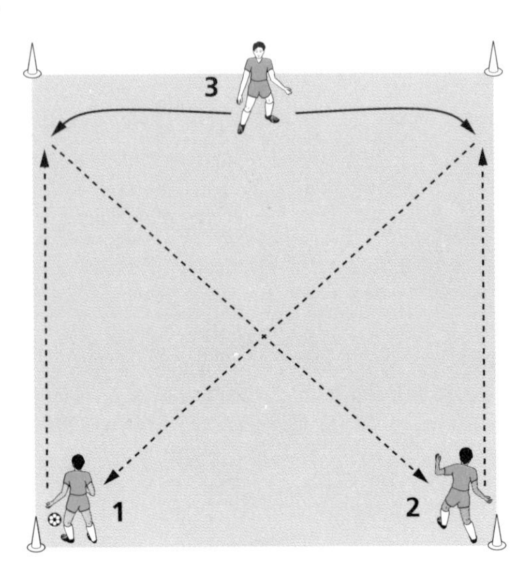

Figure 9

DRIBBLING SKILLS

Passing and moving are one way of creating space, but dribbling skills are a direct way of cutting out opponents and creating scoring chances and should be practised regularly.

Running with the ball

A wide variety of exercises to practise running with the ball are possible within four 10-yard square grids arranged in a block, as shown (Figure 10). These include: running to the centre of the square and changing direction; running with the ball diagonally (grid A); and running with the ball around the borders of a box (grid B). A shout or a whistle can be used to request a change of direction from the players with the ball.

In addition, within one of the squares, one player can stand with a ball (grid C), facing his partner in the opposite corner about 10 yards away. The player in possession dribbles the ball up towards his partner, who has also moved in so that they meet halfway. The player in possession feints in one direction (here the left), throwing his shoulder to the left and wrong-footing the defender, and then accelerates away to the right. The players then switch roles, or the drill can be repeated (grid D) with both players in possession. Make sure that the feint is practised to both left and right.

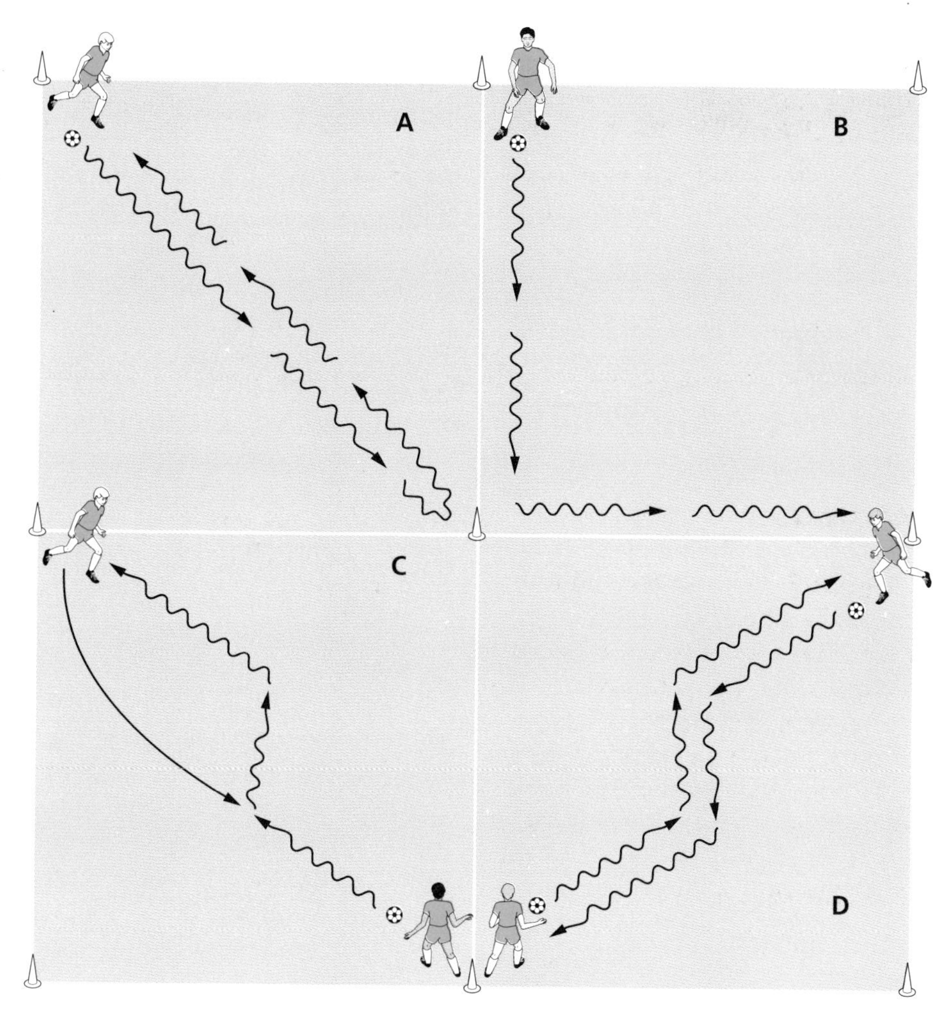

Figure 10

CONTROL AND PASS

The ability to pass accurately and quickly is obviously a key part of pass-and-move football. Controlling and passing the ball are essential skills for any young player, regardless of position, and must *always* be worked on – if you can't pass the ball, you can't play the game!

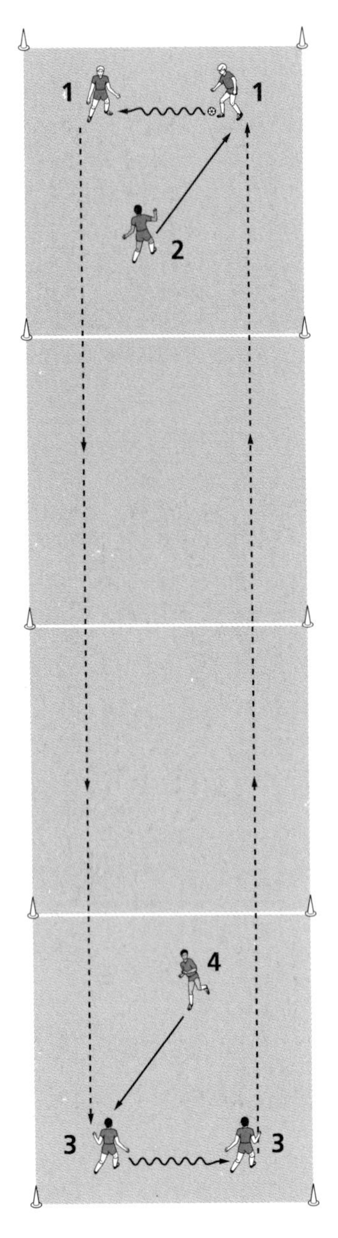

Figure 11

Driving

For this drill (Figure 11), you will need four 10-yard square grids stacked as shown. The four players start in the positions shown and the player in possession (1) moves the ball to one side of the passive defender (2) (remember that many of these drills are 'unopposed'), before driving it low over 25 yards to the player in the far end square (3). The passive defender (4) alongside the receiver lets the ball run past him. The receiver should use his first touch to move the ball to one side of the passive defender and then return the driven pass. The passive defender should remain outside the tackling distance of about 1 yard. The players alternate roles as the ball moves from end to end.

Each time, the receiver has three options. He can sweep the ball with the inside of his foot; take the pass with the outside of his foot; or let the ball run a fraction on to his back foot before pushing it wide to a new angle. In the first of these, if the ball is going to his right, he can pull it left using the inside of his right foot and then turn the right shoulder towards the ball prior to contact, driving the ball back with his left foot. To take the ball with the outside of his right foot, the player should step slightly outside the line of the ball with his left foot and bring his right foot inside the ball, while turning his right shoulder slightly to the ball prior to contact. The third technique gives the player the option of changing his mind at the last moment.

To give the ball a solid strike, the player should use a 'tight' ankle with the toes pointing down, keep the head and knee over the ball, and drive through with the instep. Young players find driving the ball quite difficult to master – hooking it is a common problem. To make good contact, the body needs to be turned slightly and the strike must be deliberate.

Control and move (1). The player prepares to receive the ball with the inside of his foot (here, the right).

With his weight on his left foot, the right is freed to make contact with the ball.

Contact is made by pushing the ball across the player's body to the left.

With the ball out of his feet to the left, he moves away to continue the movement. The whole sequence of control and move is performed as one continuous movement.

Control and move (2). The player prepares to control the ball with the outside of his foot (here, the right).

He gets 'outside' the line of the ball and, with a sweeping action, moves the ball to his right.

The change of direction is now complete and the player moves away quickly.

Control and move (3). The player gets his foot (here, the right) in line with the ball, with his weight on his front (left) foot.

On contact with the ball, the player pushes it to the right with his instep.

After pushing the ball out of his feet, he accelerates away quickly.

Triangular passing

This drill (Figure 12) develops the driven pass further and also helps to improve the players' ability to retain possession in a crowded midfield.

Using a triangle of cones, player 1 lays a straight ball outside 2's cone. Player 2 drags the ball across the back of his cone and passes to 3, who receives the ball, completes the same controlling movement and passes to 1. In time, the cones can be replaced by defenders.

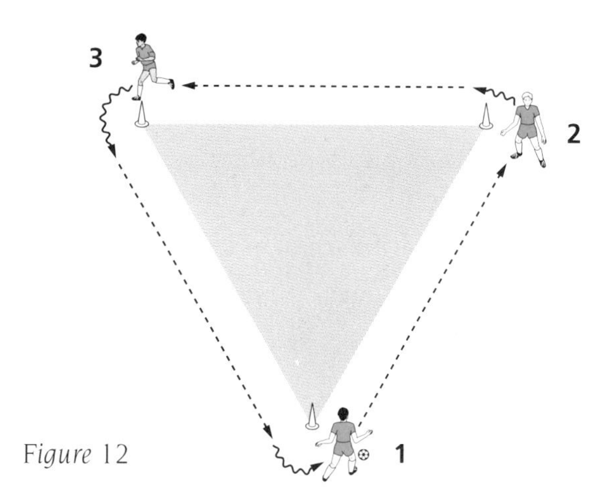

Figure 12

Two-against-one 'getting out'

This drill (Figure 13) develops the skill of finding a team-mate when under pressure. Using eight 10-yard square grids stacked as shown, two players occupy each of the end grid pairs and pass to each other without the ball landing in the middle four squares. Stationed in these four middle squares are two defenders, each looking after one end and able to move into the end zones to put pressure on the passing players.

The exercise can be made competitive, so that every time the defenders win the ball or force an error, the passing players lose a life, and every time a pass is completed the defenders lose a life. The first to lose three lives loses the game.

The two end players must work as a team and make good angles for the passes. The defender can force a player to use his weaker foot – usually the one that has a loose ankle when contact is made in passing the ball.

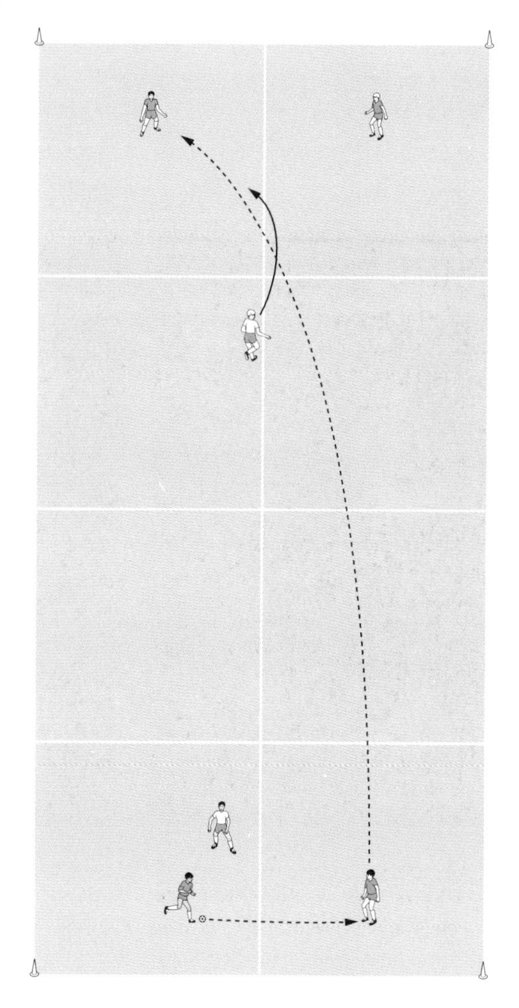

Figure 13

KEEPING POSSESSION

The modern game demands that players are skilled in keeping possession, especially when they are under pressure from the opposition and there is no team-mate in a position to pass to. But players must also be equipped to *turn* while in possession in order to make inroads in midfield and attack. A sure touch, and quick feet to wrong-foot defenders, are just two important techniques to be applied when practising these drills.

Turning himself in. From a starting position on the half-turn, the player comes to meet the ball and, instead of setting the ball back, prepares to turn by using the inside of his foot (here, the right).

After turning the ball to his left, he wrong-foots the defender and looks to move away quickly.

The player has turned himself in behind the defender with his first touch.

The defender is now completely wrong-footed as the forward moves away into the space behind.

Figure 14

Shielding the ball

This drill uses a 10-yard square grid (Figure 14). Player 3 acts as a defender standing behind 2, the player who is developing his shielding technique. Player 1, 10 yards away from 2, rolls the ball up to 2's feet and he shields the ball from the marking player (3), keeping the ball on the foot furthest away from his marker on the half-turn and protecting possession. The aim for player 2 is to touch the ball ten times or to retain possession for 15 seconds. The exercise can be made more difficult for player 2, who should use his arms and upper body to keep the defender away, if 1 throws the ball at his thigh or chest to control. In the early stages, you should restrict the defender to let the forward have the first touch unchallenged.

Shielding. Prior to contact, the player gets into a half-turned position and offers the outside of the foot furthest from the defender (here, the right) to the ball.

Using his body for protection, and shielding the ball with the outside of his right foot, he can now dictate play using the contact he has achieved.

Control on the chest. The player uses his arms to make as big a surface as possible on which to control the ball. His knees are flexed and his back is arched to aid good balance.

As the ball arrives, he relaxes his chest in order to achieve a good contact.

Turning with the ball

This drill uses two 10-yard square grids (Figure 15a). Players 1 and 4 are stationed at the serving end. Player 2 is positioned in front of a large cone (or passive defender), preparing to receive and turn before passing. Player 1 passes to 2, who receives and turns, before passing to 3. Player 1 then takes the place of 2, who joins 3, and 4 repeats the drill.

The player turning can come short to receive the ball, let the ball roll on to his back foot and then drag it around using the instep, or he can touch the ball with the outside of his foot and spin around the defender/cone.

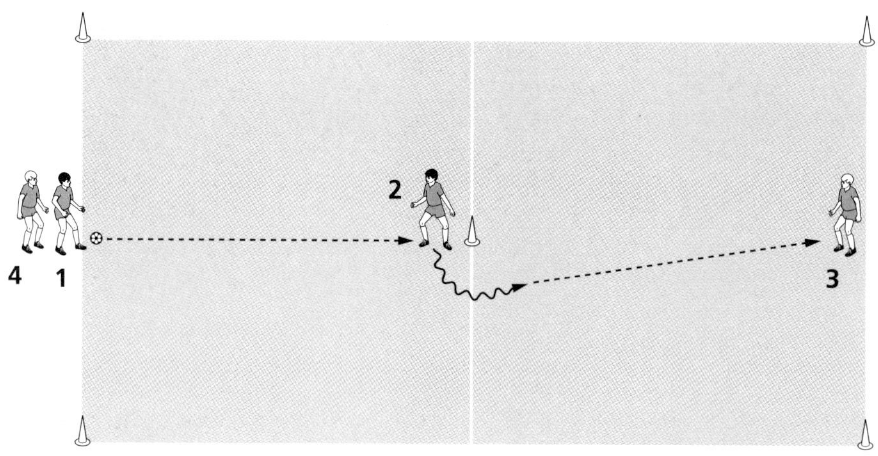

Figure 15a

The player comes to meet the ball and, as the defender tries to get the ball (here, from his left), he prepares to get his right foot outside the line of the ball.

The player moves across the defender, protecting the ball by using his body as a screen.

He rolls the ball off the outside of his right foot.

The ball is now going in behind the defender as the touch from the forward turns the ball in behind himself.

He must now accelerate away quickly in order to use the space he has created.

Using the same area (two 10-yard square grids), with a small goal stationed at the far end of the second grid (Figure 15b) where player 3 stood, the onus is on player 2 to receive, turn, shoot and score. For this skill, the player must keep a low centre of gravity, ready for when defenders are present, so that he has a springboard from which to explode away from his marker – he must not be too upright.

If there is a defender, the player can encourage him to tackle and then use his body to roll off him and away. If the ball is played to one side of the receiver, he can let it run, using his body as a shield. He can also control and beat the defender using a dribbling skill.

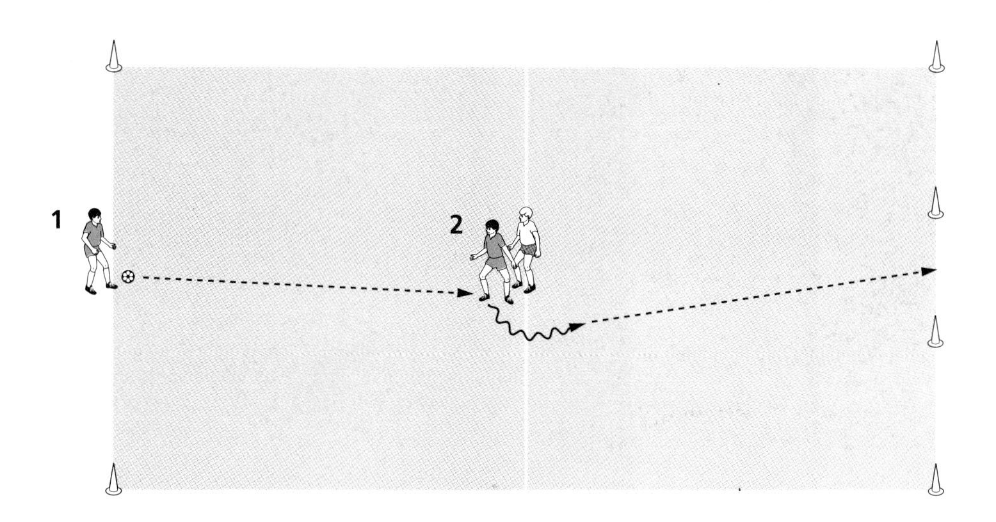

Figure 15b

Letting the ball run. When the defender gets too close before the ball has arrived, it is a great opportunity for the forward to use his body to protect the ball and let it run. Here, the forward steps across the defender as the ball arrives.

Using his body to protect the ball, the forward rolls off the defender as he allows the ball to run past him.

Using his body to protect the ball, the forward rolls off the defender as he allows the ball to run past him.

Set up and spin

In this drill (Figure 16), player 1 stands on the bottom edge of two stacked 10-yard square grids and lays up the ball at an angle to 2, who is positioned in the first grid. Player 2 lays off the ball on the half-turn to 1, who passes to 3. Player 2 spins around and follows the pass to 3, who passes along the top of the second square to 4, who dribbles down. Player 1 has replaced 2, 2 has replaced 3, who in turn has replaced 4 in his corner, and the drill is repeated.

With this exercise you are encouraging players to spin and run forward after they have set a ball back, ie 2 spins and 'supports' 3.

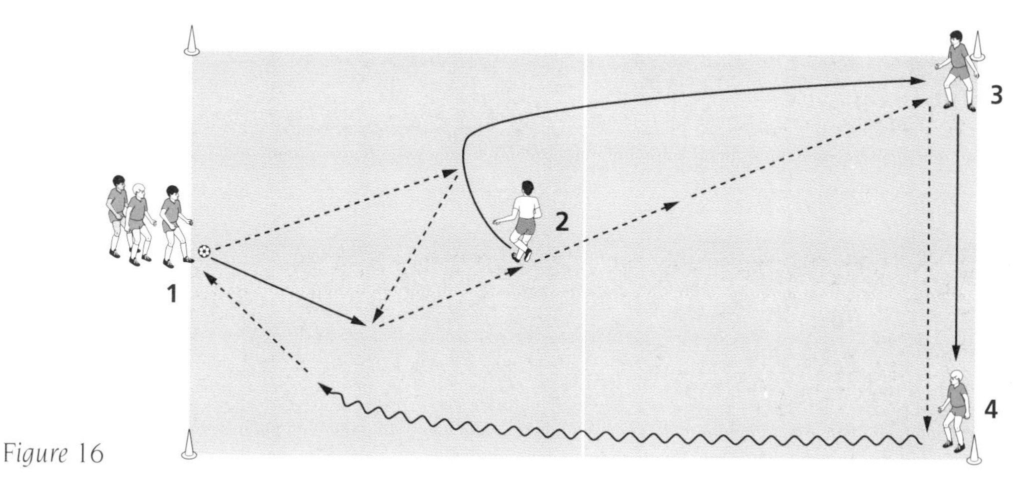

Figure 16

Turning from a defender without possession

Players also have to turn defenders when they *don't* have the ball. In this drill (Figure 17a), player 1 starts with the ball and moves to the left of 2, who is in front of a cone. Player 2 moves off the cone and turns to run behind it in order to run on to the ball played by 1. Player 2 lets the ball run across his body and, with his shoulder pointing towards the target, shoots or crosses to the far post. Player 3 also spins to anticipate the goalkeeper saving, but not holding, the shot, and he is there to put the loose ball into the net. If 1 pushes 2 too wide for a direct shot, he can cross the ball for 3. In this drill, timing is vital.

Figure 17a

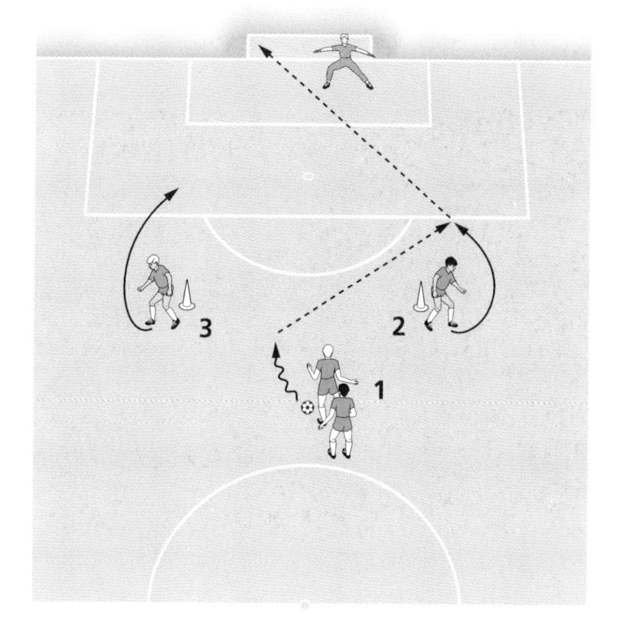

Figures 17b and 17c show how good turns can produce scoring chances in match situations. In the first situation (Figure 17b), player 1 passes square to 2, who finds 4, who himself turns and escapes his marker – in this drill, a cone – before crossing for 3, who has also turned his marker, to score.

Figure 17b

In the second situation (Figure 17c), player 2 lets the ball run on to his back foot (see the top photograph on page 72) before turning and shooting at goal himself, exploiting the space that the move has created.

By positioning your players as shown, you can alternate the drills between the left- and right-hand sides of the penalty box each time.

Figure 17c

Turning defenders

In a full match situation, attackers and midfielders must turn their markers to make space. Using a whole pitch (Figure 18a), the right-back, 1, has the open channels X and Y as options if 2 and 3 can turn their markers. The drill encourages players to play into space

Figure 18a

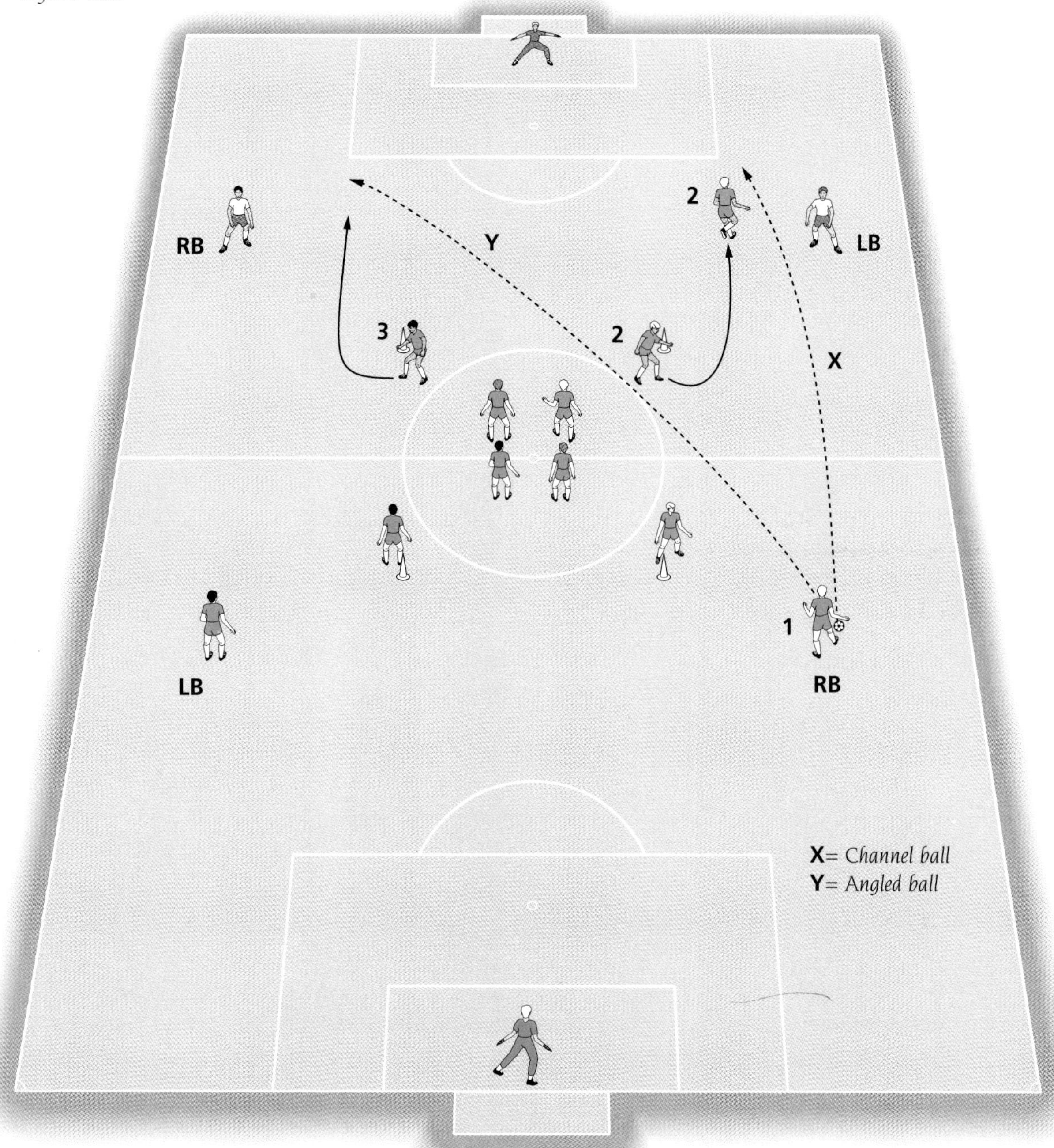

as well as to feet. The sequence can be reversed, beginning from the left.

Alternatively, players 2 and 3 can cross over (Figure 18b). As always, with offside in mind, timing is crucial, as the space that is there to be exploited is a result of the defence pushing up.

Figure 18b

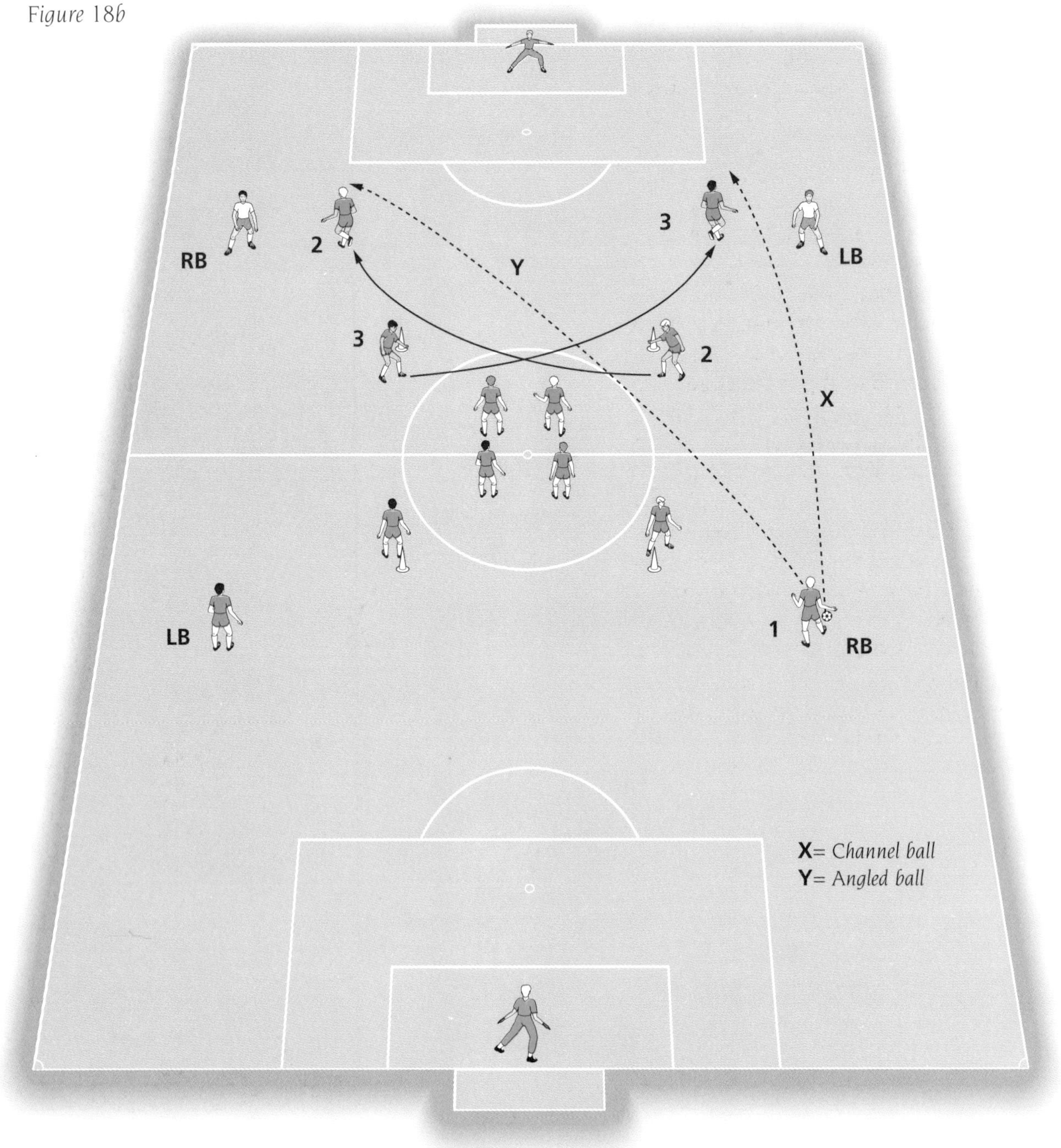

Turning two against two

The ability to hold off defenders is a skill which opens up to the coach many combinations of support play between a striking pair around the penalty area. Using ten 10-yard square grids stacked as shown (Figure 19), mark the central 10-yard strip with discs to designate it no-man's land. This area ensures that the strikers always have space in front to receive the ball to feet. Two pairs of strikers must now come to receive the ball passed over the no-man's land by their team-mates from the other half of the playing area. (A goal is scored by a pass between the cones to the feet of the waiting player.) The strikers must then try to combine to score in one of the two goals at either end of the playing area. Having scored, the defenders gain possession and feed the strikers in the opposite half and the drill is repeated at the other end. Along the sidelines of the attackers' space, six resting players act as pass options for strikers as they strive to engineer a scoring chance.

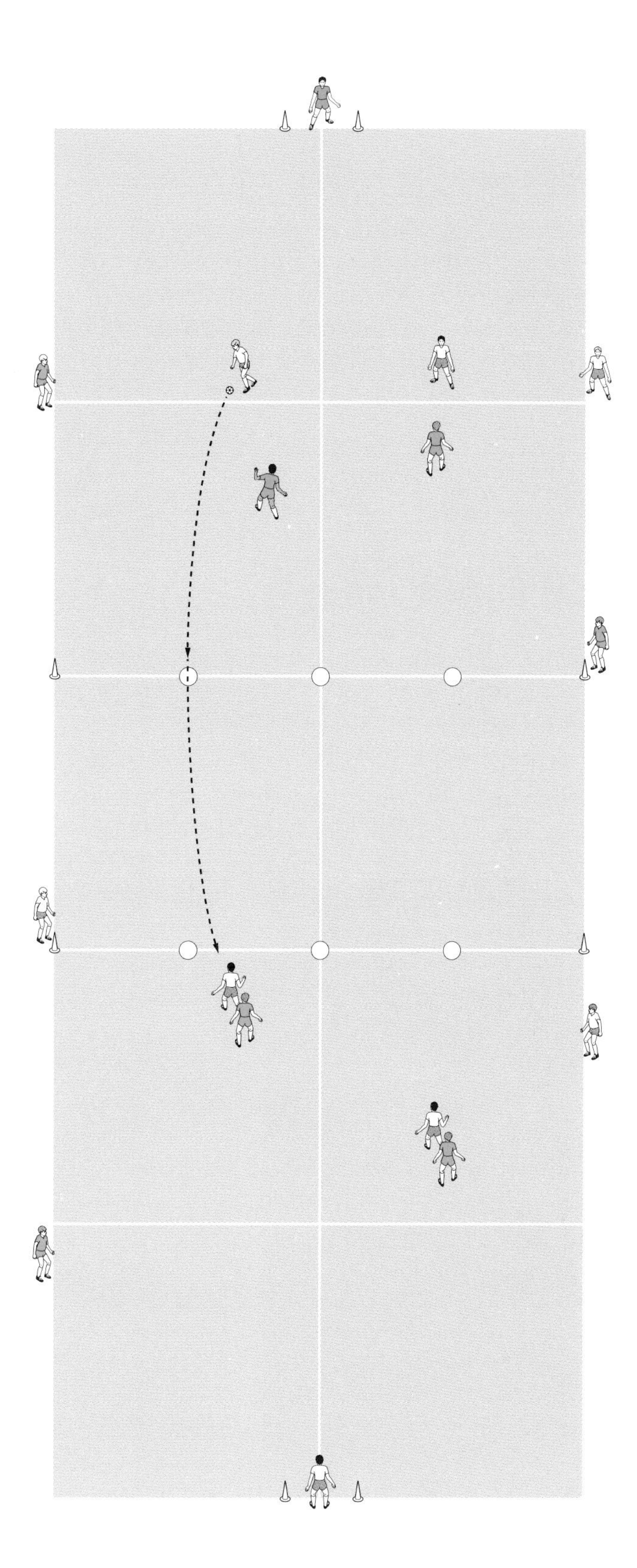

Figure 19

SHOOTING AT GOAL

Shooting at goal is essentially what the game of football is all about. Heading and volleying are two of the disciplines that young players need to practise and perfect in order to exploit good technique, passing and movement elsewhere on the field.

In these drills, watch for body shape on volleys – shoulder down and hip up. It is important to coach players to adjust their feet, shuffling backwards, sideways or forwards; read the flight of the ball before volleying; drop the shoulder to keep the ball down by getting the kicking foot into the correct position, level with the hip; watch the ball on to the foot; get good contact; and finally follow through.

Full instep volley

In this drill, four players pair off and stand 30 yards apart (Figure 20a). Player 2 serves the ball by hand to 1, who volleys it to 3 and 4, who then return the ball in the same way. Look for good body adjustment. The full volley technique requires a player to spin on, say, his left foot, and for his left shoulder to fall away while the hip rises, freeing the full instep of the right foot, with a solid ankle, to make contact. Hooking is usually the result of poor timing, striking the ball too late or poor adjustment.

The player turns his shoulder (here, the left) to the ball, creating a position of readiness.

He now 'drops' his left shoulder, allowing his right foot to make contact with the ball. His eyes are on the ball, with his arms spread for good balance.

He should try to make contact either through or slightly above the centre of the ball.

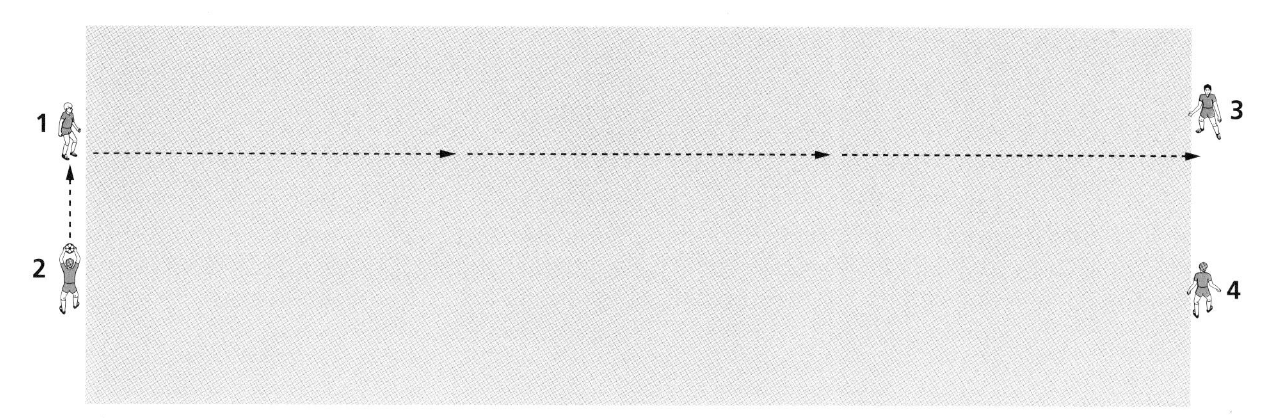

Figure 20a

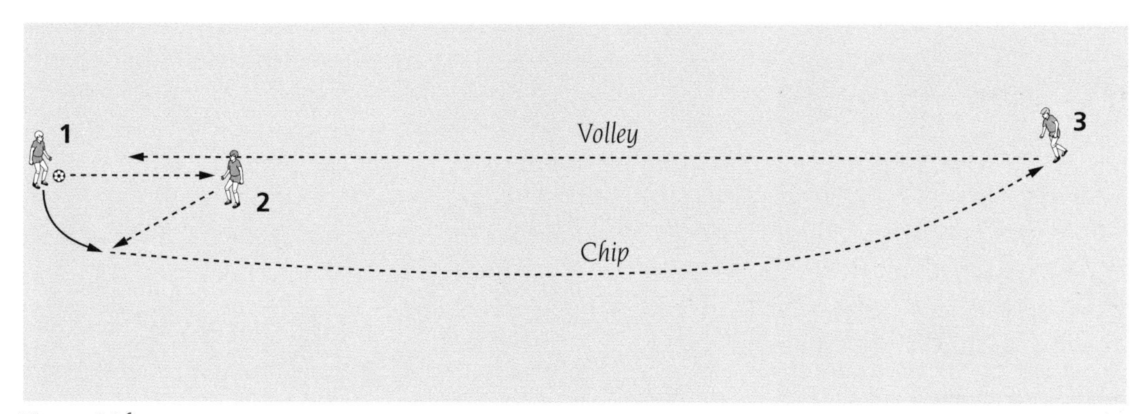

Figure 20b

Figure 20c

In a more sophisticated exercise (Figure 20b), the ball is set up for player 1 by 2 so that he can chip it to 3, using the same 30-yard space between volleyer and receiver.

In a more authentic drill (Figure 20c), balls are chipped or served from the byline to the working players, who volley into the goal from the edge of the penalty box.

Near-post finishing

In this drill (Figure 21), players form a queue back from the penalty spot with two cones in front of them, to left and right. Two servers on the goal-line loop the ball in for 1 and 2 to run on to wide of the cones and score. A passive defender can be added, but this should not dilute the thrill of hitting the back of the net with a powerful shot.

When practising this drill, remember that young or inexperienced players will want to blast the ball into the goal with power, but from close range a side-foot volley makes clean contact with the ball and is usually enough to score. The side-foot volley technique has the inside of the foot opened out facing the goal with the ankle pulled back from the knee, producing a springing action on contact.

The half-volley is a fresh challenge. If players 1 and 2 throw the ball so that it bounces, the finisher must get to the pitch of the ball to meet it on the bounce and time everything to perfection. Otherwise, he will mistime the strike, possibly losing control and direction.

You can also incorporate heading – a change of service is all that is required.

Opposite: *Near-post header. The player attacks the space in front of the defender and heads the ball in to the near post. Timing and getting in front of the defender are the prime considerations.*

Figure 21

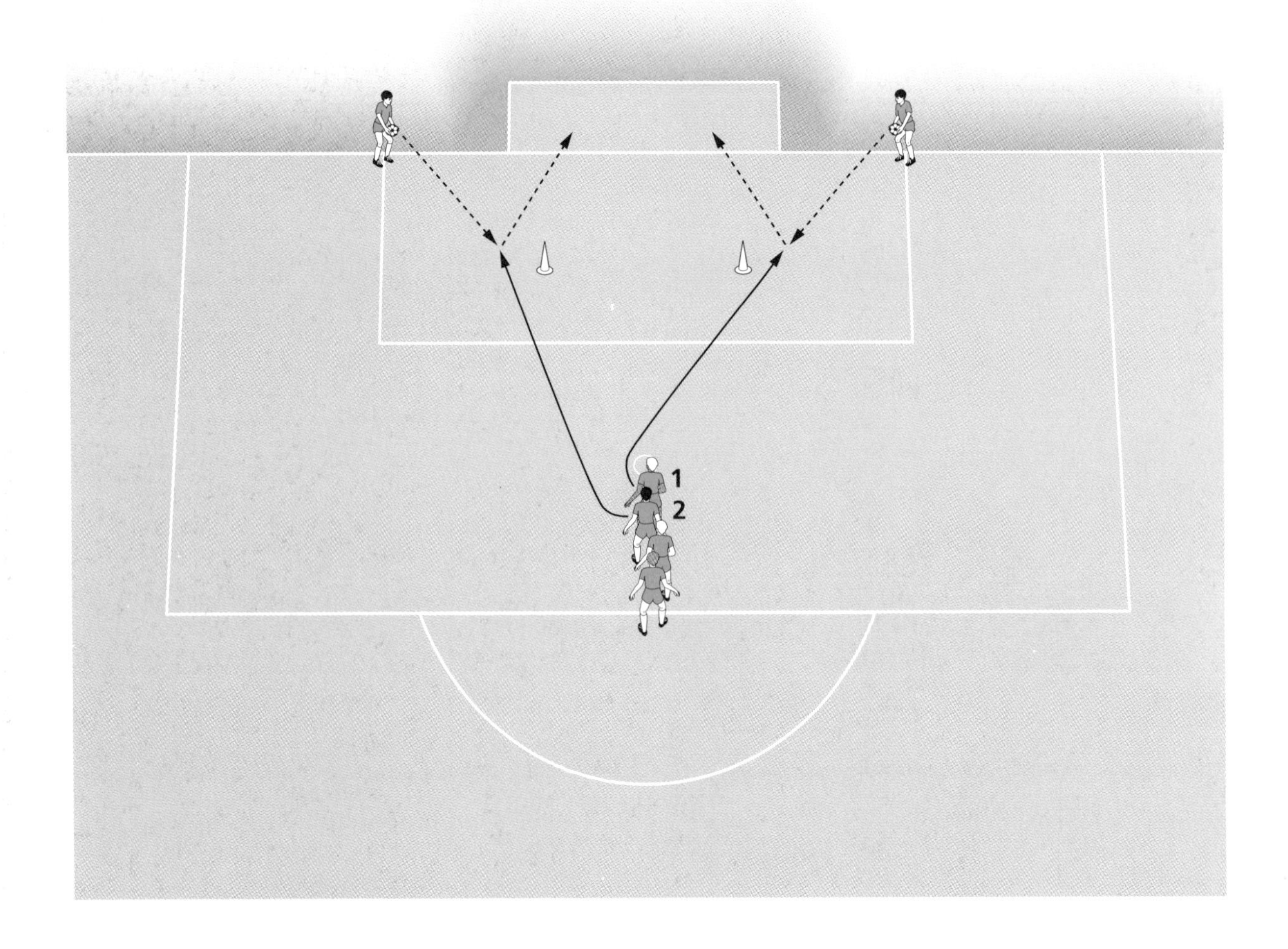

MOTORS
SOUTH EASTERN 081-
ELECTRICAL PLC 506 1717
LONGLIFE ROOFIN
TEL:0171-537 3713
PONY
PONY
PONY
LJK
FOR SALES SERVICE BODYSHOP
A Night You'll
Remember
CARLIN
CARL

Loose-ball finishing

In this drill (Figure 22), the two servers (A and B) stand on the left and right sides of the penalty area with a supply of balls. The shooters are positioned to either side of the goal, lined up from the goal-line to the edge of the 6-yard box. Player A rolls a ball along the ground in a direction away from the first shooting player, who chases after the ball, swivels and shoots. Do not allow a first touch, as pressure in the penalty area rarely allows one. Progress to a bouncing ball, still keeping to a one-touch finish.

Figure 22

IN THE GYMNASIUM

It is a misconception that the gymnasium is only for five-a-side games. Some school gymnasiums have wall bars which limit the use of the walls, but usually there are benches which can be laid on their sides to act as rebound surfaces and used to improve technique indoors (as well as for five-a-side, which are a great way to end a session!). In this section I have highlighted just a few simple practices, but with a little thought and improvisation many of the other drills in the book can be used in the gymnasium when the weather is bad.

Side-foot volley

In this drill (Figure 23), the players stand 5 or 6 yards away from the wall and practise the side-foot volley technique, allowing the ball to bounce once in tennis fashion. Hit the ball too high up the wall and it will bounce out of control; too low and it will skid back too fast. The key is to cushion the volley on to the wall with the inside of the foot, without applying any great pace, and this should be within the capabilities of most 11- to 12-year-olds.

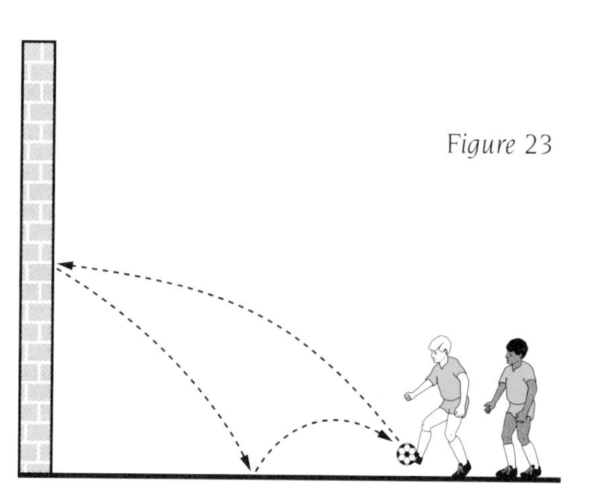

Figure 23

Turning

In this drill (Figure 24), players 1 and 2 start on one side of the gym. Player 1 dribbles the ball, drives it low at the far wall and then immediately attacks the rebound, turning on the ball and dragging it back with his back foot to face his partner, before passing the ball to 2 so that he can repeat the drill.

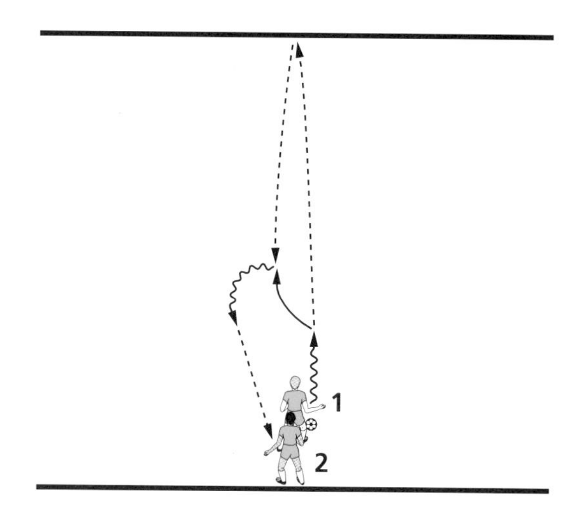

Figure 24

Heading for distance

In this drill (Figure 25), player 1 serves the ball from his hands or volleys, as shown in the diagram, to 2, who heads the ball on to the opposite wall above his partner's head as powerfully as possible. Player 2 then controls the ball off the wall and serves player 1 to repeat the exercise. In coaching this, encourage the players to achieve distance by heading with power, to use their arms to climb and to thrust their head forward at the ball.

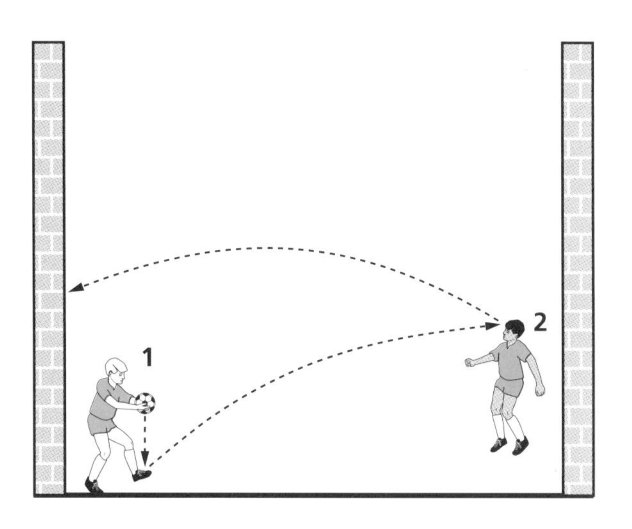

Figure 25

Defensive heading. The player jumps to attack the ball in the air. His arms are raised up to help achieve elevation and his eyes are on the ball.

As he makes contact, he thrusts his head and shoulders forward to gain power and distance.

Three against two

You can end the indoor session with three against two – one game in each half, with a goalkeeper in each goal (Figure 26). The defenders are always outnumbered by one, so whenever the ball is transferred from one half to the other by the defenders, the attackers receiving possession must all touch the ball at least once without interruption before they can score. This encourages movement and the making of passing angles, at the same time giving the defenders a chance to win possession.

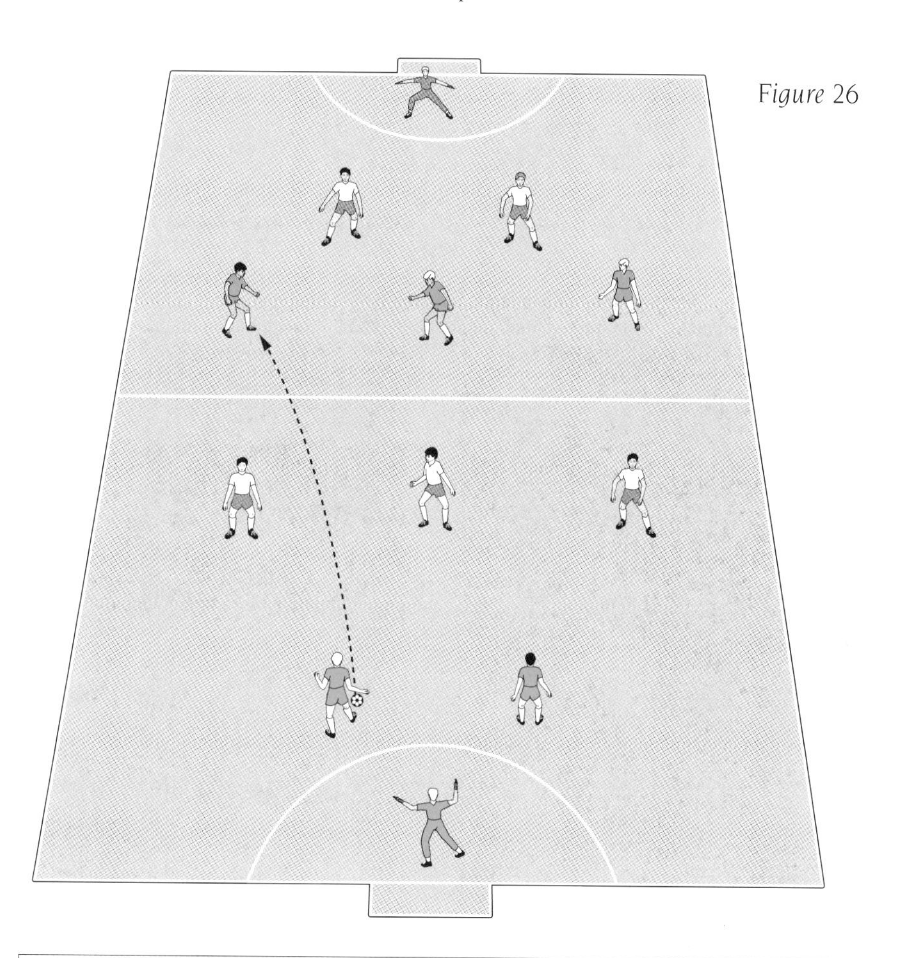

Figure 26

Conclusion

The drills provided in this section will help to establish good technique in your players, and they should therefore always come back to these disciplines whatever level they reach in the game. No player, right up to a full international, should ever neglect technique. No matter how old or experienced he is, he can *always* improve technique – it is just a matter of finding the time, or sometimes the will, to practise.

KICK RACISM
OF UPTON PARK
BRYMER
ERERS
SPORTS

2 ATTACKING PLAY

GOOD ATTACKING PRACTICES require coaches to involve at least two or three players. At any given time, only two players can be involved in passing the ball, and it is the third player, or the fourth or fifth, who must be encouraged to move and look for space beyond the passer and receiver in order to make good attacking plays. The coach must encourage players to set up plays, linking with the target man; make angles; run forward beyond the ball; pass and move, shifting the opposition around; play one-two wall passes; and play the ball first time.

Coaches will recognize that all good teams include two or three great players around which everything revolves. The AC Milan side of the 1980s, for example, had the Dutch trio of Ruud Gullit, Frank Rijkaard and Marco Van Basten! Even in a team of six, playing a small-sided game, there will be one or two players who make the difference. Patience is frequently a neglected quality in these players, but the success of attacking play lies in waiting for the right moment to trigger movement.

Every coach is looking for one or two players who will take the initiative and spark things off. The drills that follow should help you to develop the ability in your players to trigger attacking plays. Through the regular use of these practices, you will be helping them to learn to make the right choices, to try to pass with disguise, and to trigger the pass or move which creates a good scoring opportunity.

Turning on the back foot, triggering forward movement. If the defender is slow to close down the forward, the forward – coming off on the half-turn – lets the ball run on to his back foot (here, the right).

Using a dragging action with the inside of his right foot, the player swivels on his left foot to leave the ball in front of him.

The player has now turned and, with his team-mate looking to run forward, the player on the ball may look to pass the ball forward, in behind the defenders

KEEP BALL AND SUPPORT PLAY

The improvement of the physical and athletic aspects of the modern game has reduced the space available for players to keep the ball. More than ever, coaches at the top clubs recognize the importance of *possession*. The exercises that follow are designed to improve your players' ability to retain possession by supporting each other, and to develop attacking positions from good possession.

Three against three

Using four 10-yard square grids arranged in a block as shown (Figure 27), in this drill three attackers try to retain the ball against three defenders, with four supporting players on the borders of the enlarged grid offering assistance to whichever players have the ball; they are limited to one touch and can pass only once to each other. The three defenders will always be near the ball and the outside players come into play frequently, particularly when the team in possession are all marked. The players inside

Setting up the ball and making a wide angle. Player 2 passes up to his team-mate, who is poised to come and meet the ball.

the grids are coached to make fresh runs and angles that will enable them to retain possession.

A common fault when supporting the man on the ball is for the player to run at him in a straight line, thereby closing up the space and passing angles. The space between players in possession is the most vital space on the pitch: the player on the ball and the supporting player should keep the space as large as possible for as long as possible, and the supporting player should therefore make a wide angle with the player on the ball. This also moves the defender who is marking him and opens up the passing space behind them both.

This drill will teach players the value of playing through the opposition, a skill which in the 11-a-side game cuts out defenders and produces scoring chances.

Figure 27

The receiving player, who has come off on the half-turn, sets the ball back to the original passer using his back foot (here, the right). Note that the supporting player makes a wide angle, creating space for the next movement.

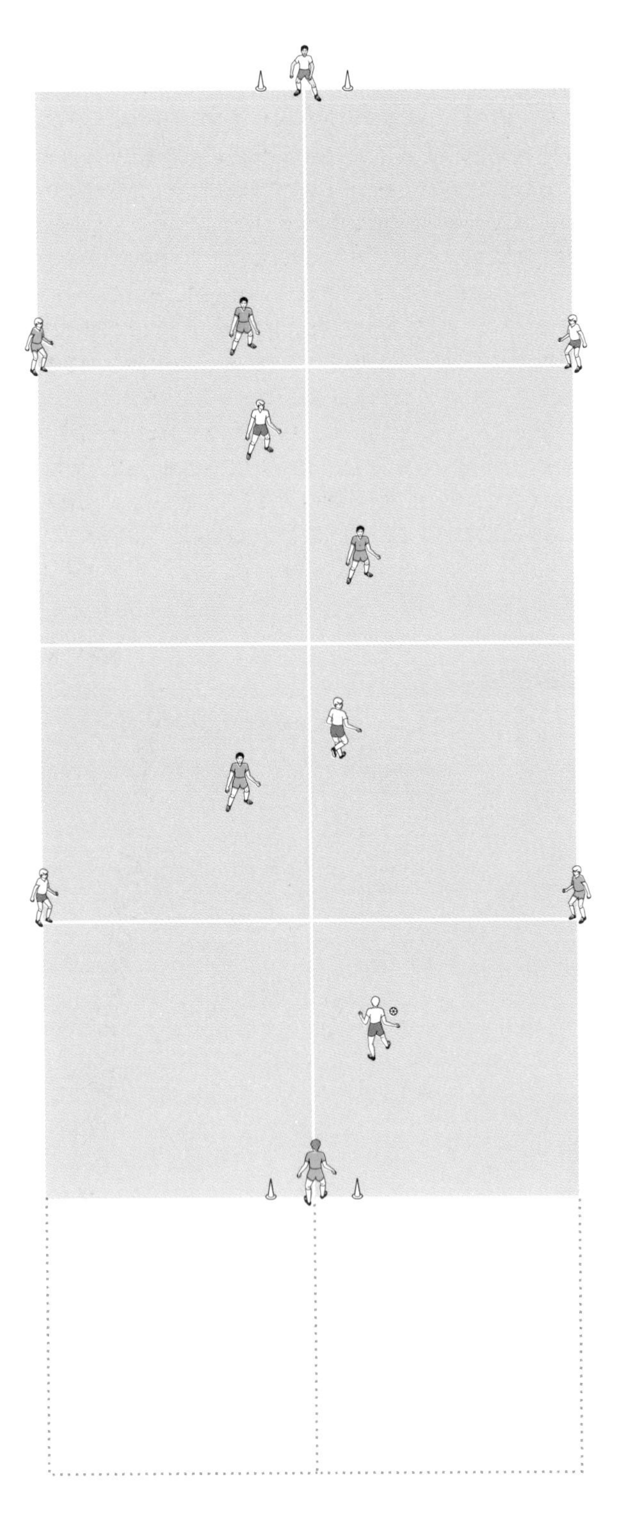

Three-against-three score and keep

This is a two-stage drill. For the first stage, use four pairs of 10-yard square grids stacked as shown (Figure 28). Twelve players are involved – six working in the grids and six resting on the outside – who rotate. At each end of the 'pitch' there is a target man.

A goal is registered every time a pass is made to a target man. When they score, the team of three retains possession and attacks the opposite end. They must do so quickly to try to exploit the other team's defensive weaknesses which will have arisen from their being occupied defending the other end. This will encourage concentration and alertness from the defending three.

In stage 2, using an area extended lengthways by 10 yards, target men stand in the four corners, which makes defending by crowding out an end impossible as there is too much ground to cover. When a target man is found, he transfers the ball to the nearest opposite corner, and the game then continues with the scoring team retaining possession and endeavouring to find a target at the other end. Having two 'goals' to attack will encourage the forwards to move the point of attack away from crowded areas. You can also add another two players (four against four) in this stage.

Figure 28

Half-pitch game

This drill uses a strip in half a pitch (Figure 29), with coloured discs marking out an imaginary halfway line. Twelve players are divided into two teams of six; each team has three defenders and three attackers, who stay in their own 'halves'. In both halves, the defenders mark down the opposing three forwards. The six players on the outside are split into three on each team to offer support to their respective team-mates, with a goalkeeper at each end.

In the drill, the ball is transferred from the defenders or goalkeeper in one half to the forwards in the other, who try to score. You can make it a condition that all the forwards must touch the ball before a shot can be made: this forces players to move, change their positions and create passing angles. It also encourages the three forwards to support each other, cross over, make little dummy runs off each other, demonstrate good close control and create movements to get shots in, while at the same time improving their technique. If at any given time a forward is in trouble and isolated one against one, he can use any of the support players to keep the movement going.

Primarily, this is an excellent practice for attacking, but it is also good for defenders. Whichever defending system is employed in the practice – 'zonal' or 'man-for-man' – the coach should ask himself: 'Who has lost his man? Who has lost his concentration? Who watches the movement and forgets the ball? Who watches the ball and forgets the movement?' You will find more defending drills in Chapter 7.

Figure 29

Seven-against-seven keep ball

In this drill (Figure 30), the pitch is partitioned off for a game of seven-against-seven. A team scores a goal if it links eight consecutive passes, and continues in possession until the ball is given away. The drill highlights the importance of players *looking*. I urge them: 'Get a picture. Head up, head up. Keep the ball moving.' Quick passing is rewarded – the old adage 'You can't tackle a moving ball' is applicable here.

Figure 30

Breaking out from the back

This drill requires 15 10-yard square grids stacked three by five (Figure 31), giving an area 50 yards long and 30 yards wide which is divided into two by discs. Three defenders play against two attackers in each half. All three defenders have to touch the ball before it can be played to one of their forwards in the other half. Once the two forwards receive the ball, they must combine to try to score.

Figure 31

The three defenders are coached to make their passing area large; create wide angles; play between the two attackers as one defender breaks behind them into a forward space; find their forwards; and stay in support.

The defender who is spare can join his two attackers, creating three against three in the other half (although the attackers themselves should be restricted to one half). This encourages confidence in bringing the ball out of defence. All too often, defenders are content just to hoof the ball up the pitch: this drill stresses the importance of building up moves from the back.

If the ball is given away, the defender who has joined his attackers must retreat quickly, but the defence in possession must still all touch the ball before they try to exploit the poor defensive positioning that they may face if a defender has joined his attackers. The attackers must be encouraged to track back to the halfway line.

The coach must make players aware that, during 11-a-side matches, when a player breaks out from the back and runs into the midfield area the central midfield players have to split, making passing angles. One may run forward, creating a running target. The decision for the defender is whether to keep running, pass to midfield, or pass to a striker or running target. The decision lies with the player on the ball, and through practice and experience he should be able to make the correct choice himself.

The progression from Figure 31 is to lengthen and widen the pitch to add a central area, introducing four midfield players. The drill now has defending, midfield and attacking thirds. The defenders can break forward as before, as can one attacking midfield player. The drill becomes more match-like, but still defines the roles of the three areas: defence, midfield and attack.

COMBINING TO SHOOT

Interplay between two or more players is what creates space in the modern, 'tight' game. To set up attacking plays that end with a shot, coaches need to encourage players to combine with each other.

Blind-side reverse pass

This drill uses the last third of the pitch (Figure 32). Player 1 passes the ball square to 2 and then runs diagonally behind the cone (representing a central defender). Player 2 controls the ball on his back foot and passes into the path of the running 1, who has moved into the inside-right position on the edge of the penalty area. Player 1 then cuts the ball back into the path of 2's right-to-left diagonal run, which mirrors 1's initial thrust. Player 2, in possession, can now shoot.

Players can over-use the square ball, but here it exploits the blind-side run, which itself exploits a situation where a defender is watching only the ball. Even at the highest level, defenders have a tendency to ball-watch: sometimes it is only for a fraction of a second, but it gives the runners a chance to create a goal-scoring opportunity.

Figure 32

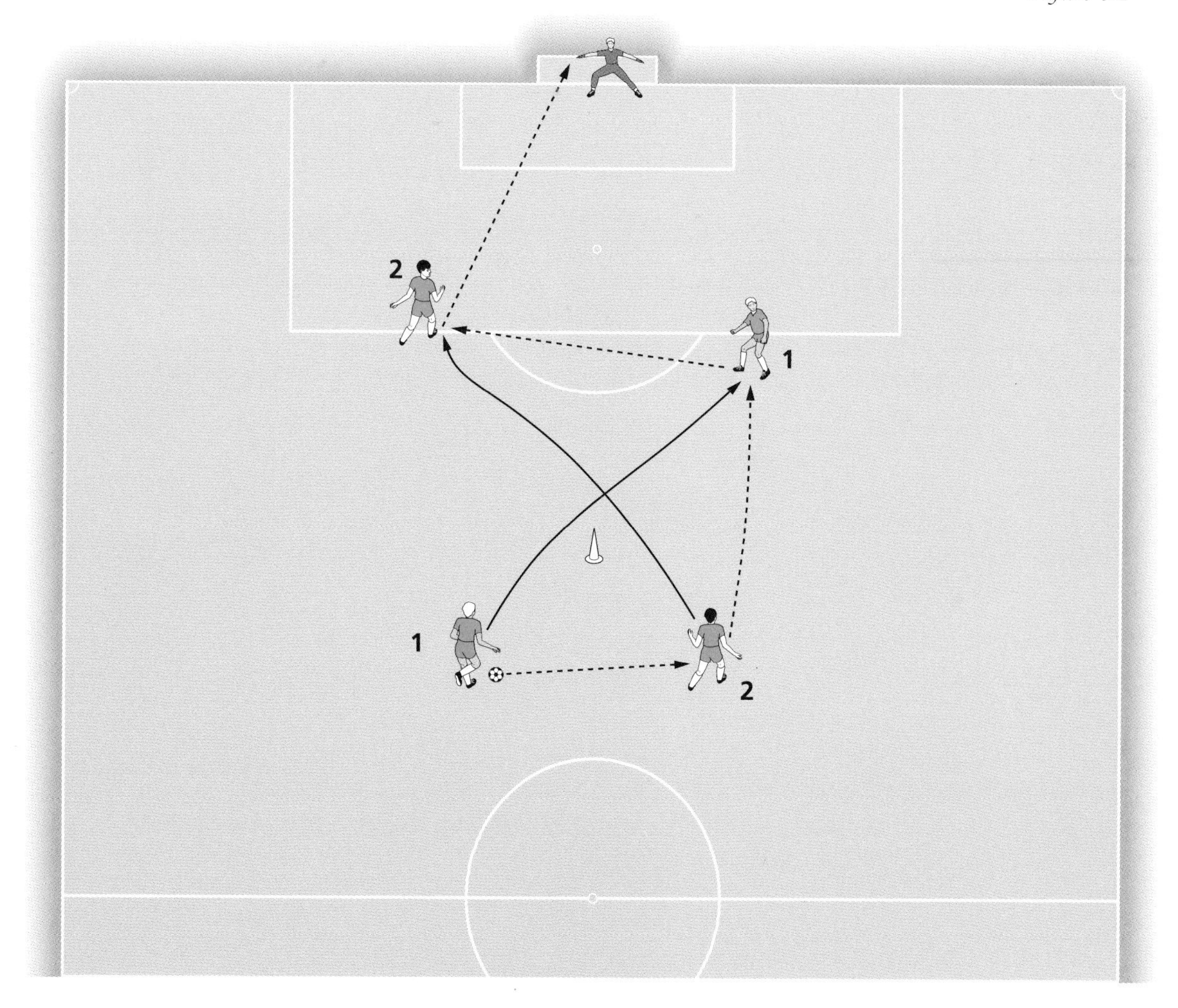

Blind-side run and finish

This simple practice can alternate down either wing. In this drill (Figure 33), it is down the left side of the pitch in the final third. Player 2 runs with the ball just inside the large cone and the wide player, 1, makes an angled, blind-side run around the back of another cone. Player 2 passes the ball in a straight line behind the cone to 1, who picks up the ball, takes it to the byline, and cuts it back to the penalty spot or the edge of the box for 3 and 4 (the constant strikers) to shoot, preferably first time. Players 3 and 4 should combine to give 1 attacking options.

The blind side run by player 1 must not be made from a standing position. His run must be made in relation to 2, who initially has the ball. As 2 starts to run towards the cone (mimicking the defender), 1 should pull away from his 'defender' and then run forward behind him as 2 passes the ball.

Timing is important: in a full-scale match, offside is always a consideration.

Figure 33

Supporting inside

This drill (Figure 34) can also be alternated down either wing. Its aim is to utilize the skill of playing the ball with the outside of the foot to a support player. Player 1 prepares to lay the ball up to 2. Player 2 turns away, then checks back towards 1 running slightly outside the path of the ball, offering the outside of his right foot to the ball. Using the natural curved surface of his foot, he knocks it on to 3, the front striker, who has come short and then sets the ball back right-footed into the path of 2 who has followed his pass, arcing inside the line of the ball, and is on the edge of the penalty box looking to shoot first time.

Swapping roles can give all the players a greater understanding of the routine. Player 1 becomes 2, 2 becomes 3, 3 collects the ball and joins the original queue, and 4 becomes 1.

Figure 34

Late run from midfield

This drill, with the pitch set up as shown (Figure 35), starts with the goalkeeper throwing the ball to the feet of player 1, who passes to 2 on the left wing. Player 3, who has initially supported his right-back, 1, turns and runs to arrive in the penalty area late. Player 2 crosses into the path of 3, who tries to score. The players can move on one place to interchange roles. Again, the drill can be alternated down either wing: reverse the procedure for the other end, passing goalkeeper to left-back, to outside-right, to midfield.

Figure 35

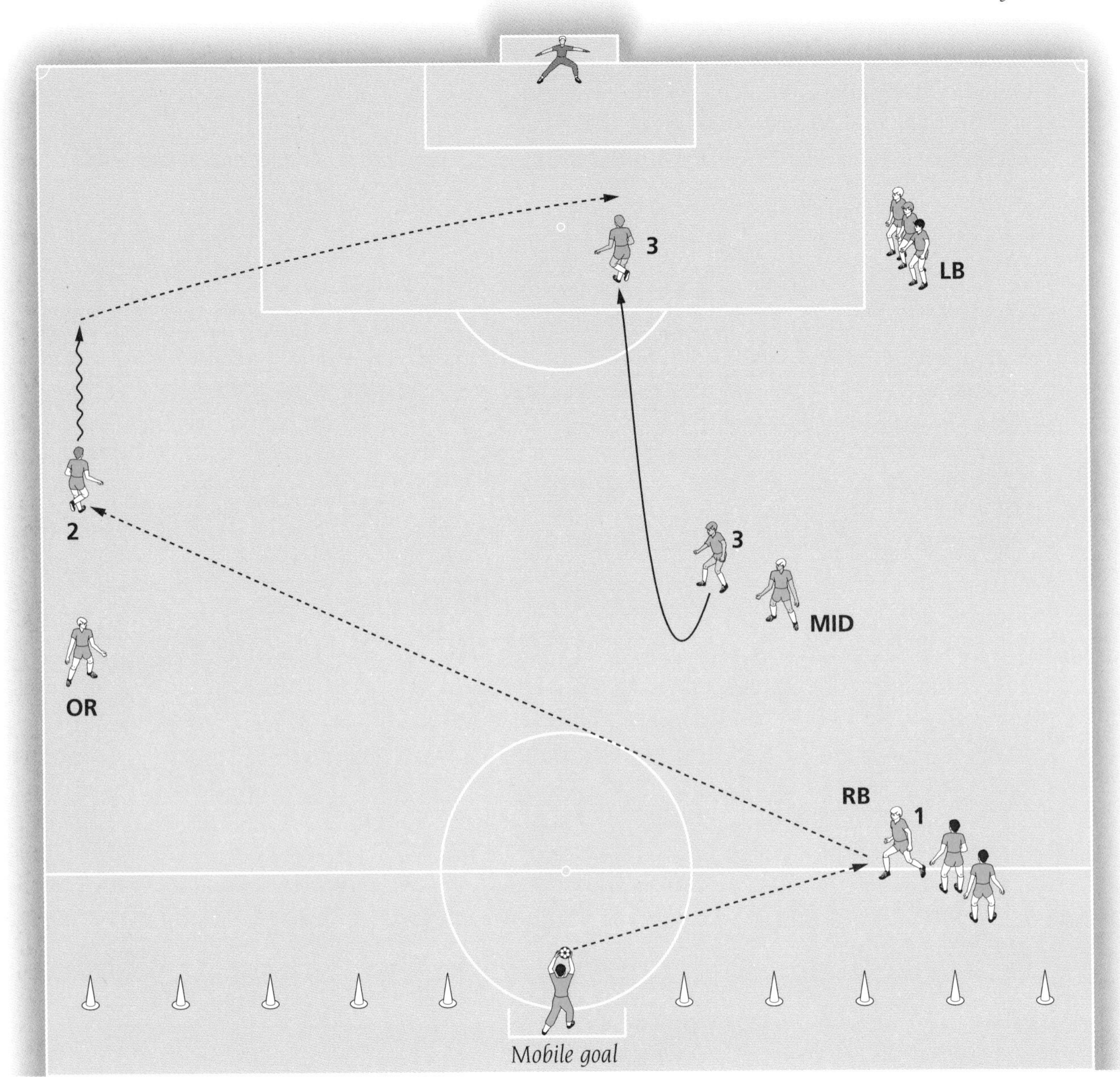

Take-over combination

This drill (Figure 36) encourages combinations to develop. Player 1 passes on one side of the cone to 2, who controls and screens the ball while 3 begins to run across him. Player 2 either slips the ball to 3 or carries on his own run and shoots at goal himself.

Figure 36

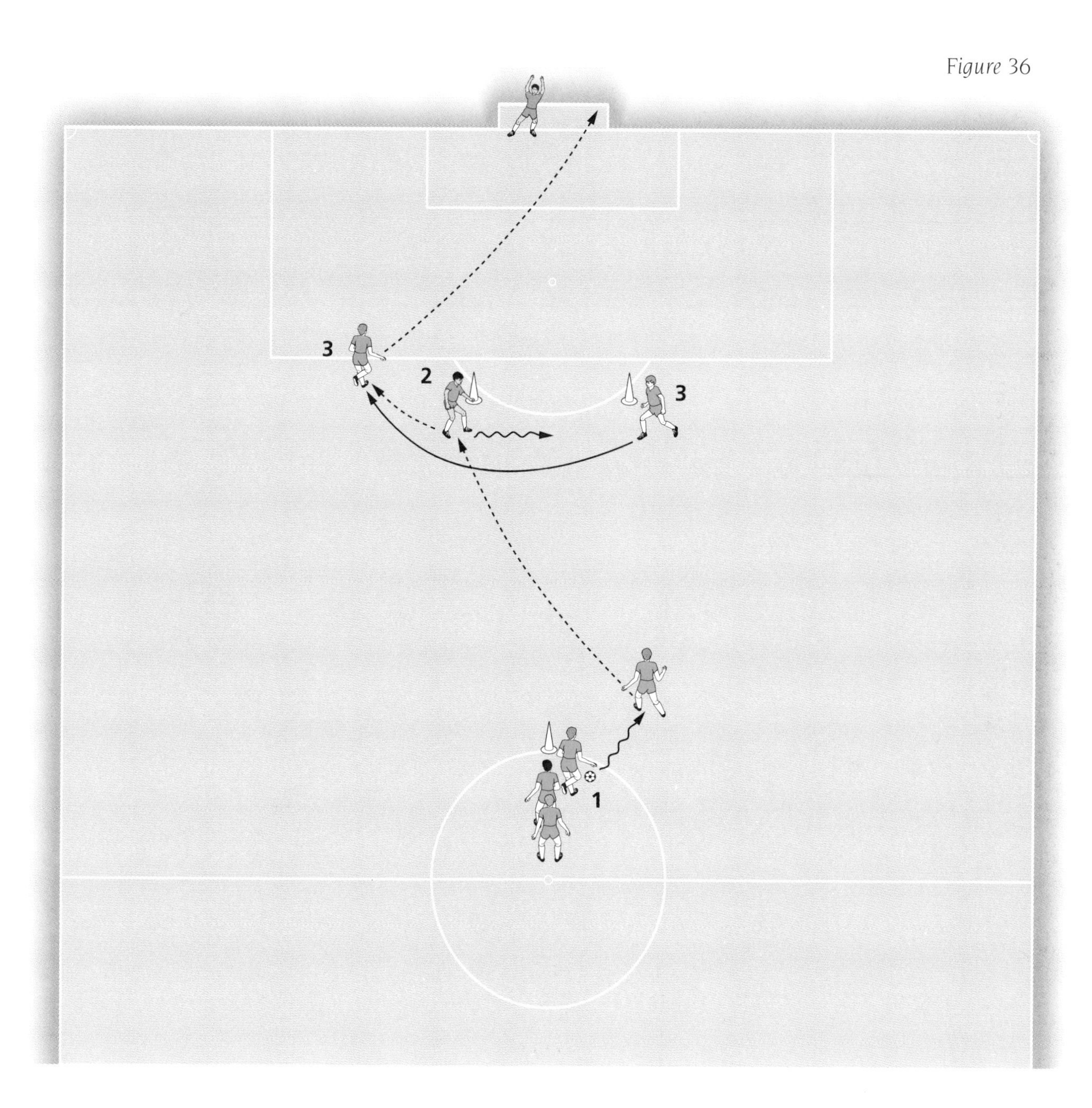

Take-over run. The player in possession shields the ball around the edge of the penalty area. The player off the ball starts to make his run.

The player on the ball moves towards his team-mate and manipulates the ball with the sole of his foot.

With as much disguise as possible, the player on the ball rolls it with the sole of his foot into the space for his running team-mate.

The ball is exchanged and the take-over move takes place.

The take-over has created the space for player 8 to shoot. Timing and speed of movement are essential in order to fool the defenders.

'Dummy' take-over. The player in possession 'dummies' to use the player who is running across him.

With a quick movement, he now completes the disguise and takes the ball for himself to shoot at goal. The run of the player off the ball is used to fool the defenders.

Strikers cross-over and play wide

A wide player can also be involved (Figure 37). Player 4 runs down the wing to receive the ball from 3, before crossing near or far post to 2 or 3. Players 2 and 3 must be quick and accurate, and perform the practice with pace to exploit the space their movement has created. The drill can be alternated down either wing, and variation on the crosses needs to be encouraged.

Far-post header. The ball is hung up to the far post and the player jumps high to make contact with it. His arms are up for balance and his eyes are on the ball, directing it down.

Figure 37

Finishing on the near post. The player attacks the space on the near post where the ball has been played. By timing his run in relation to the cross, he arrives in the space at the same time as the ball.

Using his outside foot (here, the left), he guides the ball into the goal past the stranded goalkeeper.

Conclusion

You will never recreate a match situation on the training ground, because it cannot have the same edge and, in formulating attacking play, players get artificial space. However, you can coach the team to attack in a certain way, and the defending team can be asked to simulate the team shape or system of your next opponents, thus making the training match-specific.

For example, Figure 38 shows how the attacking team can be prepared to play 4–4–2 against 5–3–2 (although in this drill it is not 11-a-side), which is the system of three centre-backs used at Liverpool, Chelsea and Aston Villa. This is done by playing 'attack versus defence'. Only one goal is attacked; one 'team' of eight or nine defends while one 'team' of nine attacks. The basic formations are there but you are playing nine versus nine or nine versus eight. (With young players, you may need to overload with an extra attacker – nine versus eight.) This allows your players to practise attacking plays such as overlapping full-backs, for which they have already been drilled, against a formation they are likely to encounter in a match situation. Another option to practise is the long, angled ball towards the second striker to isolate the far defender.

In exploring these options, you are still focusing on playing your own game, and passing the ball to give good depth and penetration. But you are using the whole pitch so that all options can be considered, not just moves in isolation. This style of practice can be expanded to full 11-a-side games, where there should be signs that the work in training can be transferred into real matches – which is the whole point of coaching.

Figure 38

DAGENHAM
MOTORS

3
'THIRD MAN' RUNNING

THE ART OF 'third man' running (Figure 39) is the key to the West Ham pass-and-move way of playing football. It is what gives this style the thrust eventually to penetrate defences and create scoring chances. With young players, you will be trying simply to develop the basic habit and understanding of 'third man' running. It is then up to them to introduce it when they feel the situation is right.

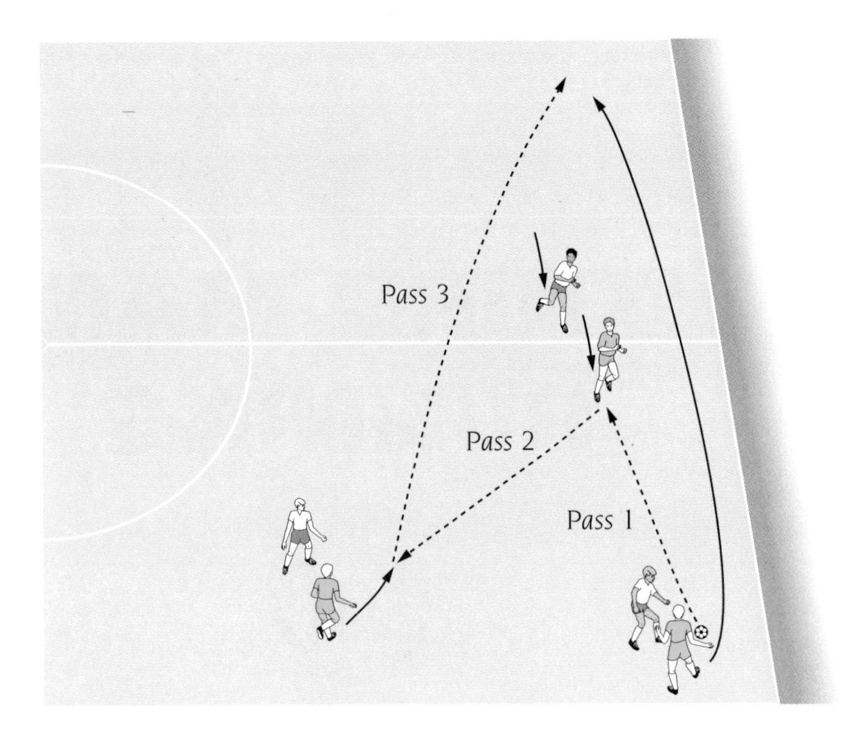

Figure 39

GENERAL MOVEMENT

The drills in this section will develop your players' ability to move off the ball and to see where space can be exploited by a run or pass.

Overlapping

In this drill, three players stand in a slight arc 10 yards across (Figure 40). The middle player, 1, passes the ball to the player on his right, 2, and follows the pass behind 2 on the overlap. Player 2 collects the ball and angles his pass left, in front of 3, the wide left receiver. Player 2 now overlaps around the back of 3, who continues the sequence by passing to 1, who has become a wide man. The tempo can be increased gradually.

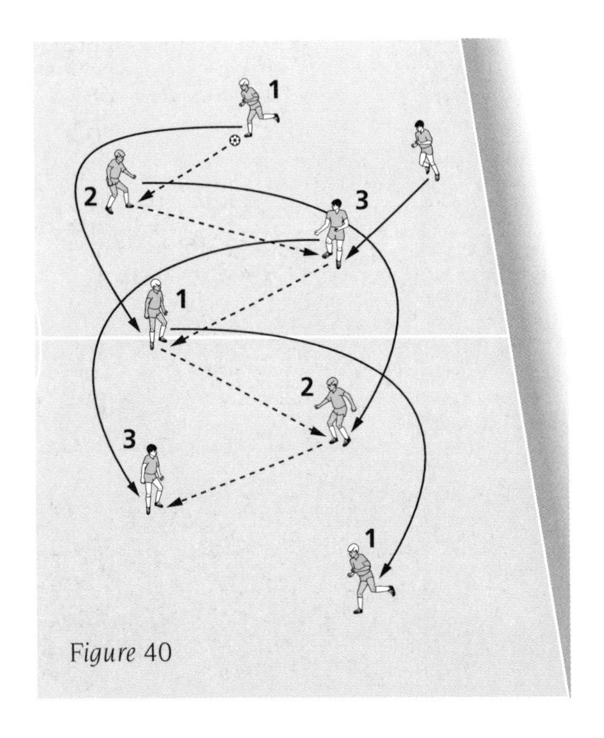

Figure 40

Triangle

In this drill, the three players start in a triangle (Figure 41). Player 1 passes the ball to the target, 2, and runs wide of the pass. Player 2 lays the ball off the back foot to 3, who finds the run with an accurate through ball to 1, the 'third man', who has reached the new target position. Players 2 and 3 then become the support players and the exercise is repeated.

The target man should be slightly on the half-turn and should be able to knock back the ball with his first touch, so that it can be played behind him and into space at speed.

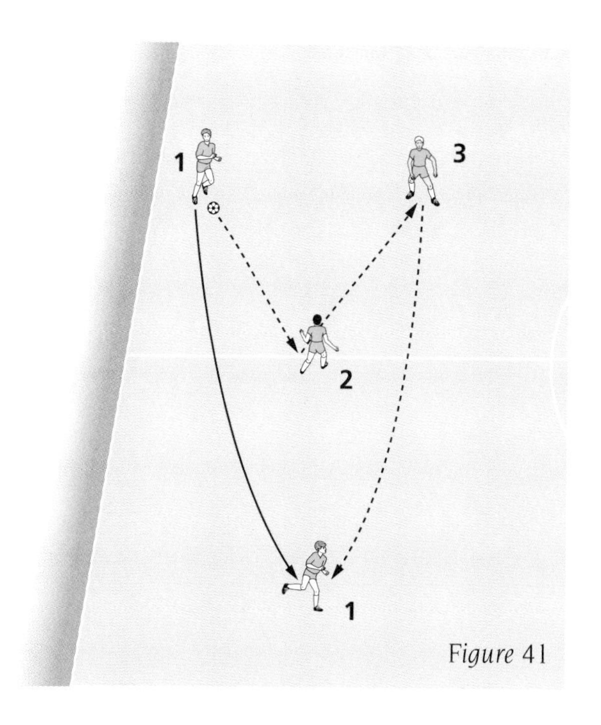

Figure 41

The half-turned starting position. The near player stands slightly half-turned: from here, he can see the defender, and will be able to move quickly into any position.

Laying square

The square ball can be the start of a more penetrating move. In this drill (Figure 42a), players 1 and 2 stand apart at the base of the triangle supporting the apex, 3. Player 1 lays the ball square to 2, who passes to 3. He in turn picks up 1 on the run, who then finds 2, the 'third man' running forward.

To repeat the drill, the 'third man' runner becomes the target – player 2 takes the role of 3 – and the move progresses until it reaches the borders of the training area. A good coach can break down the drill into simple parts for young players, who may find it too complicated at first.

Many variations are possible. Instead of playing the ball back to player 1, the target man, 3, can pass back to the same player who gave him the ball (2 in Figure 42b). The overlapping player, 1, does not receive the ball from 3, so he adopts the role of 2 and makes the 'third man' run himself.

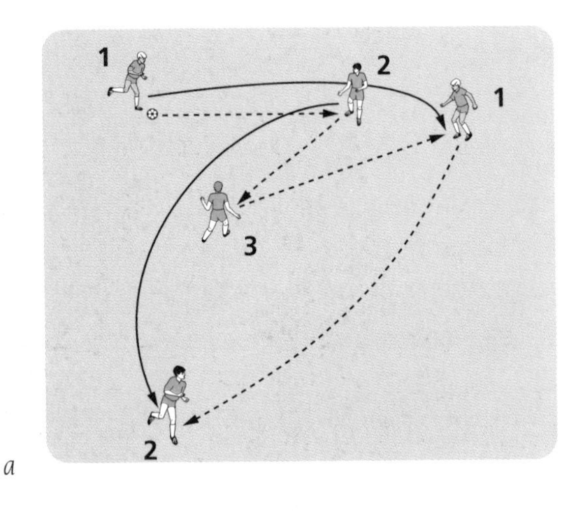

a

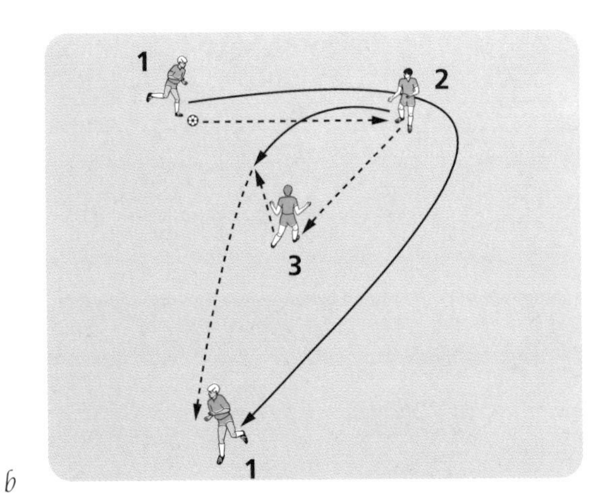

b

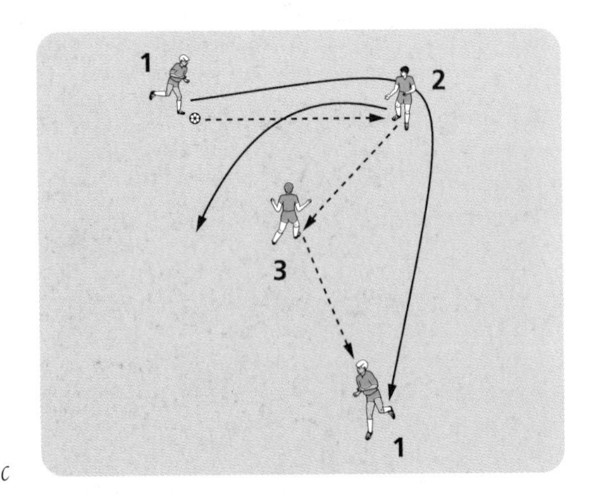

c

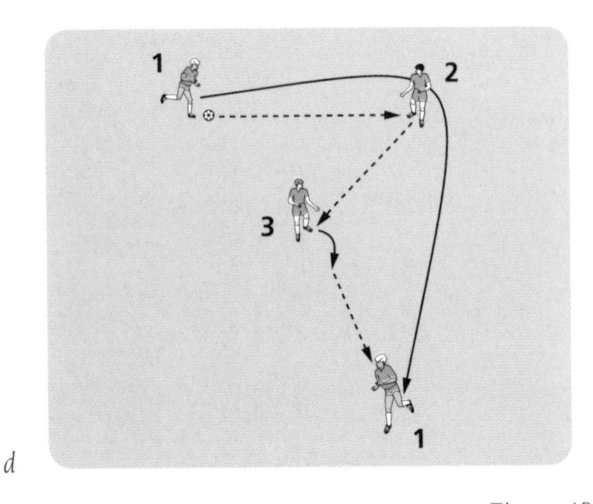

d

Figure 42

Other options include a flick to the runner (Figure 42c), where player 3 holds the ball while 1 runs and is found with a forward pass from the flick of 3's boot. Player 2 still runs to support. Alternatively, player 3 turns on the ball and slides it to 1 even further ahead (Figure 42d).

With players making the quick decisions required for good football, mistakes and misunderstandings will inevitably occur. This drill aims to improve technique and understanding, but its primary message is that 'third man' running is the key to 'making something happen'.

Good technique is crucial. Depending on the situation and position of opponents, the ball may have to be chipped, pushed along the ground, passed with the outside of the foot or curled with the inside of the foot in order to find the 'third man' runner. The 'final ball technique' (the ball into the runner) will be up to the individual and will depend on the situation that confronts him.

The coach's priority is make players understand that the game – and particularly one-touch football – is played *off the ball.* The theme of 'third man' running will recur again and again in this respect.

The end product of 'third man' movement

Passing with the outside of the foot. The player places his standing foot (here, the right) well outside the line of the ball, in order to create the space for the outside of the left foot to make contact.

After contact, which should be made on the outside of the ball, the player follows through with his leg – this will create bend/curl on the ball.

should be a cross or a shot at goal. Figure 42e shows examples of how these drills can be adapted to a full game situation. It may not be the same three players who are involved; it may be just two strikers making the plays. But the basic premise is that you can coach three players to make any movement happen anywhere. The rule to observe is that if there is movement 'once the ball has been set up it must go behind or wide'. If not, keep possession and be patient.

Figure 42e

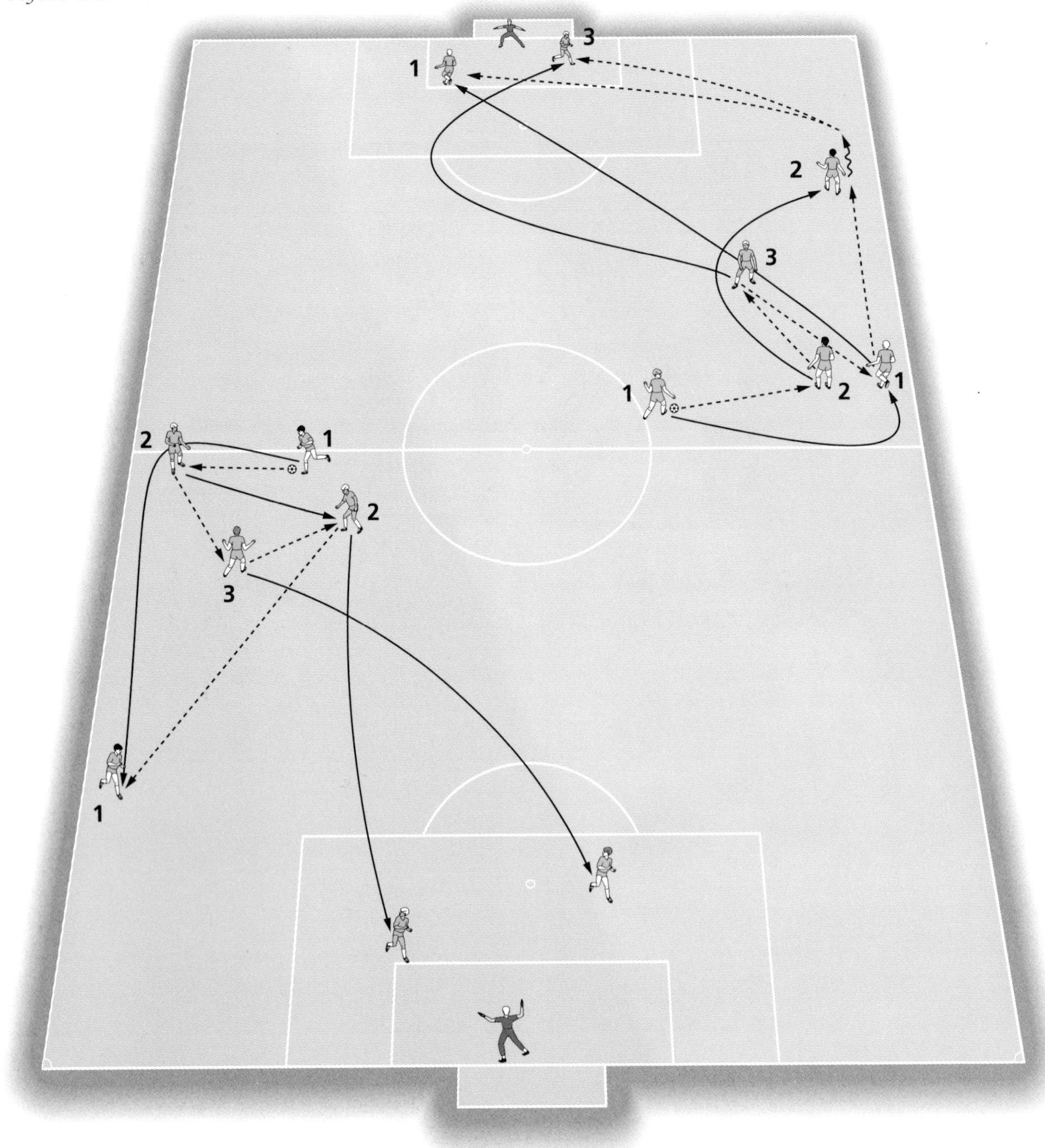

Striker set-up

This drill (Figure 43) requires plenty of running off the ball, using a marked-out area 60 yards long by 30 yards wide (grids are not necessary). The target men/strikers (players 5 and 6) stand on the halfway line, near the touchline. From close to the centre of the base, player 4 receives the ball square from 3 and with a long pass finds 1, who lays off the ball to a supporting player, 2. This prompts players 5 and 6 to make their runs in order for 2 to pick them out with a pass, chip or volley.

The ball must be played in front of the strikers, who should both run as if they are losing a marker. In reverse, players 5 and 6 become 3 and 4, and 1 and 2 swap roles.

The skills that this drill develops include the ability to kick the ball accurately to a player standing and facing the passer 30 yards away; to receive the ball from that distance and lay the ball back; and pass into space, in front of strikers on the run. It also helps players to improve their timing, as with offside in mind the timing of the runs is crucial.

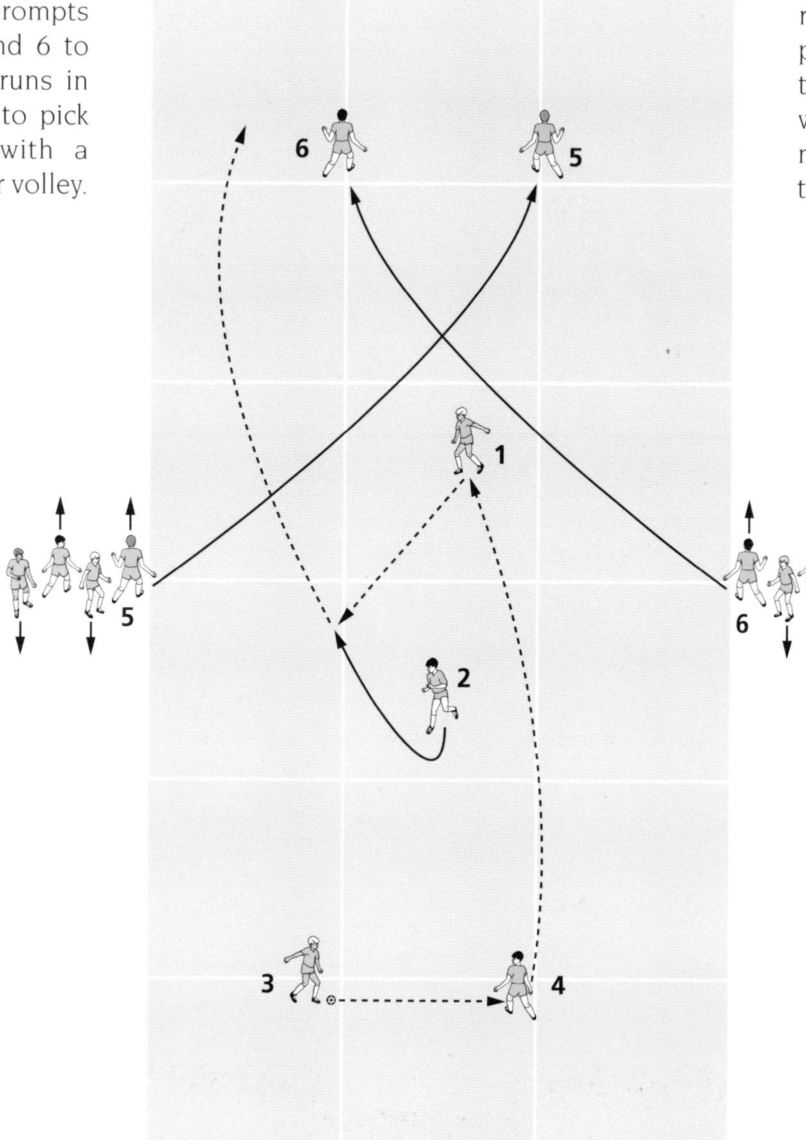

Figure 43

Midfield running

Figure 44 shows two moves that will help to develop 'third man' running in midfield, with players on the half-turn laying off the ball to exploit space ahead. If you use a full pitch, it will help illustrate how the moves would work in a match situation.

In the first move, the left-sided midfield player, 1, passes to the feet of the central striker, 2, who comes to the ball and lays it off to the central midfield player, 3. This player can then pass the ball into the space behind the central striker for 1, who has made a 'third man' run.

In the second move, player 3 finds 4, wide and at an angle, who sets back the ball to the supporting left-sided midfielder, 1. As player 4 prepares to receive the ball, 3 runs across the pitch – a blind-side 'third man' run – and 1 finds him in space behind 4. Both drills should finish with a shot on goal.

Figure 44

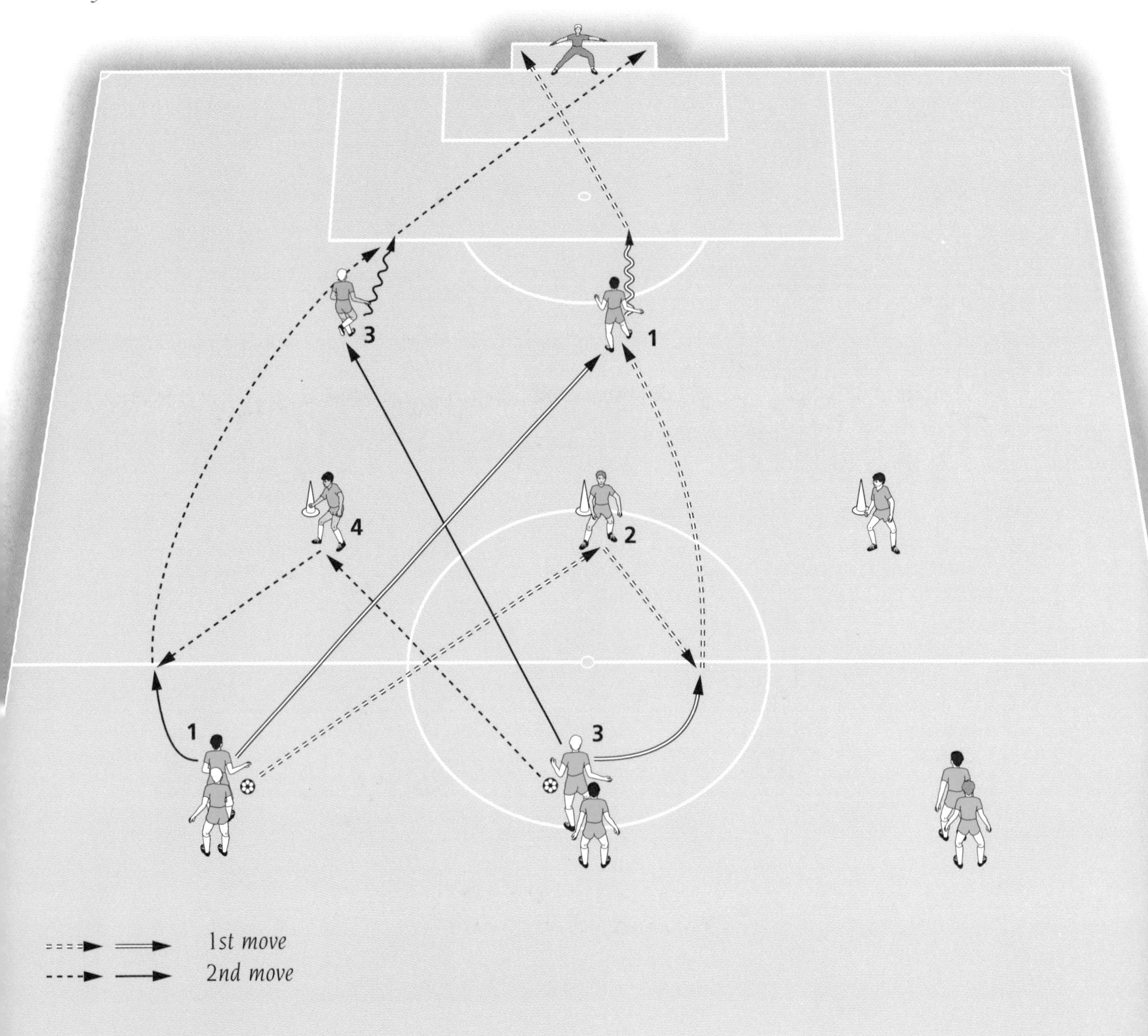

Two runners

In this drill (Figure 45), player 5 has two runners as passing options. Player 4, in the defensive half, passes to 3 who finds 5, who either passes straight in to 1 – who has made an angled run from left to right – or angles a pass in to 2, moving from right to left. Sometimes the long angled pass has to be driven or chipped into space, because the ball must be lifted over the defending players. The cones represent the defensive line and the runners must avoid being offside.

Following the first drill, player 4 becomes 1, 5 becomes 2, and 3 remains as the target. The roles of 5 and 4 are reversed.

Figure 45

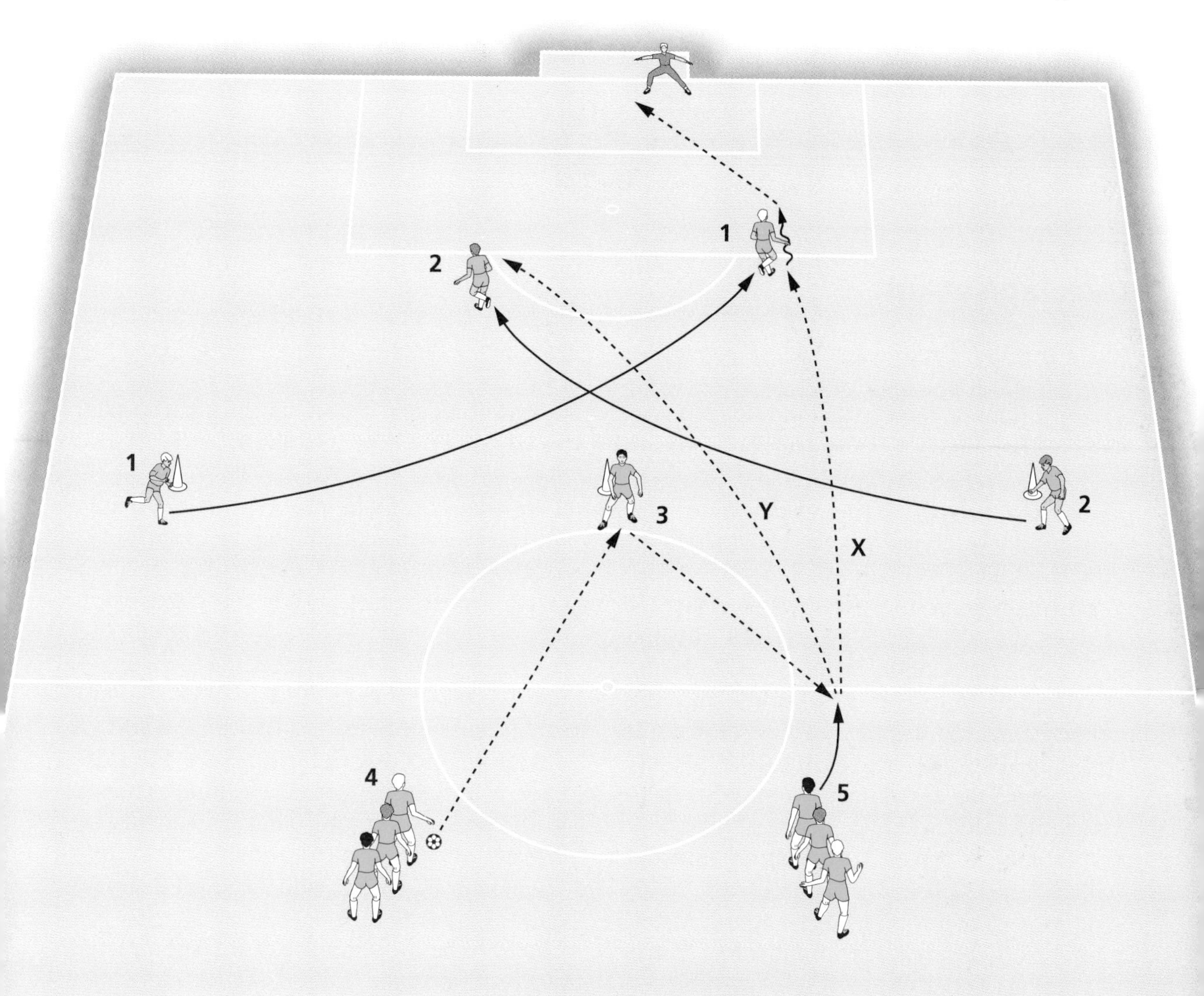

X = *Straight ball for runner 1*
Y = *Angled ball for runner 2*

BALL CIRCUITS

The philosophy behind the unopposed technical work of combination plays, or 'ball circuits' – practices that can flow until the coach halts them – is that you are coaching young players to put together three or four skills in matches such as setting up play, overlapping, one-touch passing and running with the ball, finishing up with a shot at goal. You may, for example, have been practising near-post finishing situations in isolation: in a ball circuit, the striker could receive just that type of ball from an overlapping player.

As the players progress and the practices are speeded up, with opposition added in later, the technique and movement which makes up a ball circuit will be reproduced instinctively – and ultimately in match play. Ball circuits allow the coach to bring two movements together and the practice to flow continuously, as in a game.

Overlap/set-up

These two ball-circuit exercises (Figures 46a and b) feed off one another to give the coach a continuous practice. In the first move (Figure 46a), player 1, the right-back, passes to 2, the right-sided midfielder. Player 2 passes the ball to 3, the right-winger, and overlaps. Player 3 controls the ball, takes it in from the touchline and passes to the striker, 4, on the edge of the penalty box. Player 4 receives the ball from 3 and passes into the path of the overlapping runner, 2. After laying off the ball to player 2, 4 spins into the penalty box, joining the waiting (constant) striker, 5. Player 2 crosses into the penalty area, where the two targets, 4 and 5, run to attack the ball.

The winger, player 3, can either turn the ball into the striker with the outside of his right foot, or control it with his right foot and play it with his left. The midfielder, 2, has the option of controlling the ball with his left foot and then passing with his right. The striker, 4, can control with his left foot and pass with his right.

When the movement has been completed, player 1 becomes 3 (full-back to winger), 3 becomes 2 (winger to midfielder), 2 becomes 4 (midfielder to striker), and 4, who has shot or ended up in the penalty box (as the additional striker), joins the queue for the start of the second practice.

In the complementary practice (Figure 46b), player 1 lays the ball up to 2, who sets it back to him. Player 3 anticipates that 1 is going to pass it first time and comes short to receive the ball. Player 2, the midfielder, supports the ball from 1 and makes an angled run inside the line of the ball to be available to 3. Player 3 passes the ball to 2, who then passes it into a wide area where the right-back, 5, or right-winger, 6, is waiting to receive it. The wide player runs on to the ball and can cross to 3, who has run from midfield, or 4, the (constant) striker, who has turned and run into the penalty box.

When the movement has been completed, player 1 becomes 2 (full-back to midfielder), and 2 becomes 3 (midfielder to target). Player 3 joins the queue at the start of the previous practice, while the queue for this drill provides a new player 1.

Figure 46a

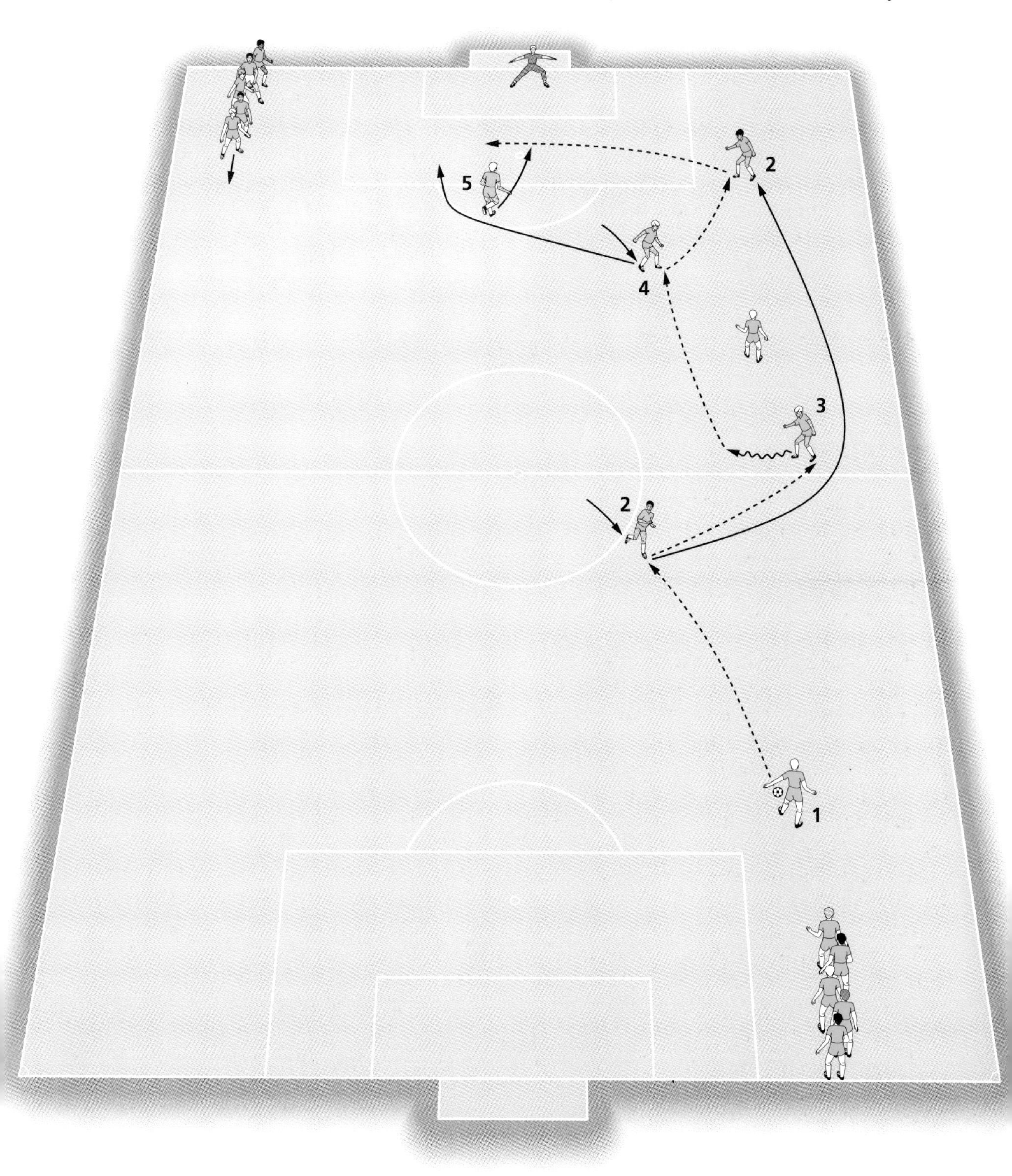

Figure 46b

Playing out

This ball circuit allows players to practise bringing out the ball from the back, using the whole pitch. In the first drill (Figure 47a), the spare players queue to lay the ball up to the right-back, 1, on the corner of the penalty box, who chips it to 3 (a striker who could have come to the ball to receive it), who sets it back to 2. Player 2 passes the ball on to the running wide player, 4, to cross for the twin strikers, who make split runs to the near and far post. The players then rotate positions: a spare feeder player from the queue becomes 1, 1 becomes 2, 2 becomes 3, 3 becomes 4 and 4 joins the queue of spare players for the complementary exercise (Figure 47b).

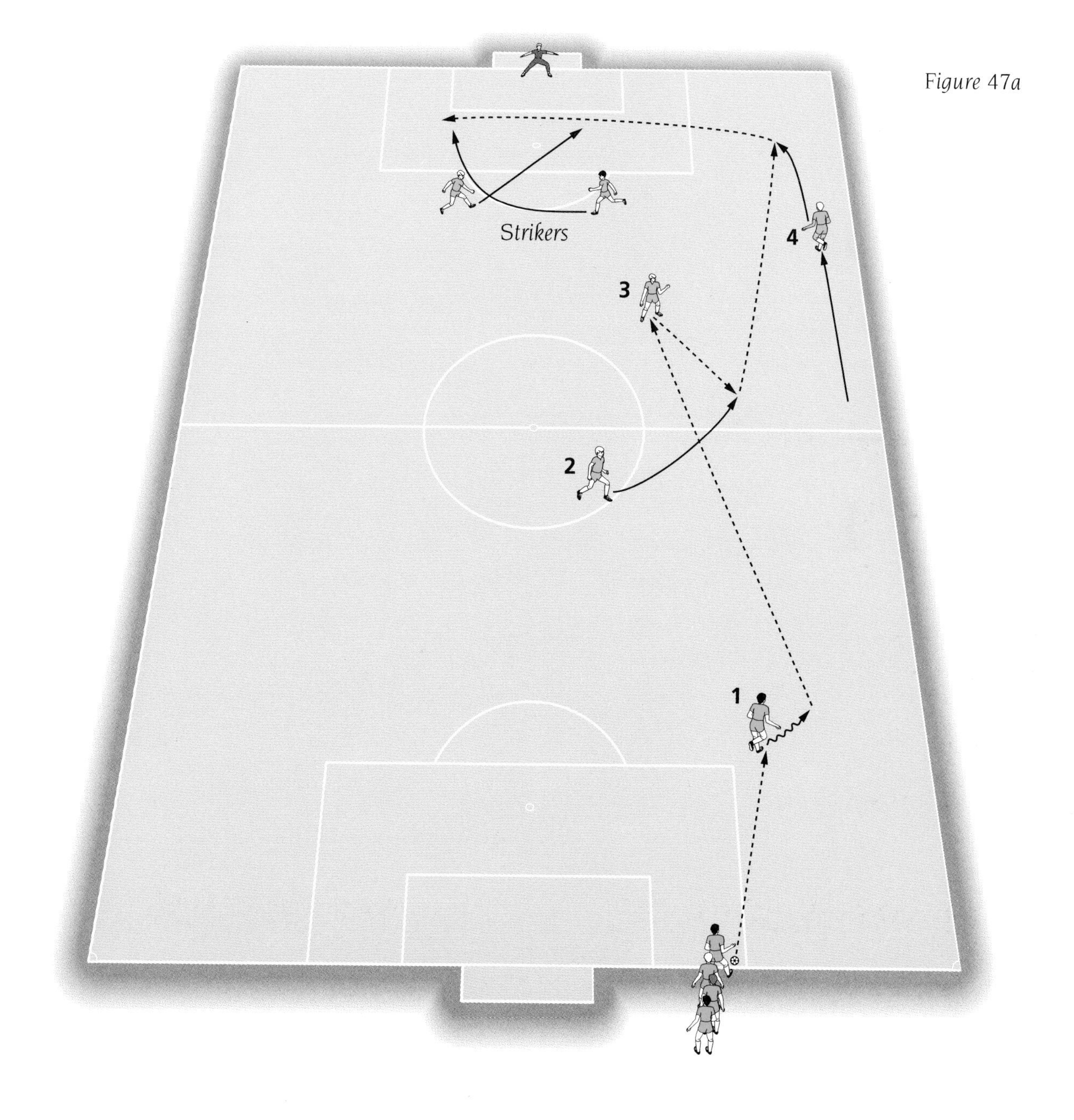

Figure 47a

In the second drill (Figure 47b), the full-back, 1, finds 4, who sets it back to 2. Player 3, who has come short, spins and turns to run on to a pass from 2, before crossing to the twin strikers, who again make split runs. A spare player from the queue then becomes 1, 2 becomes 3, 1 becomes 4, 4 becomes 2, and 3 joins the queue for the other drill.

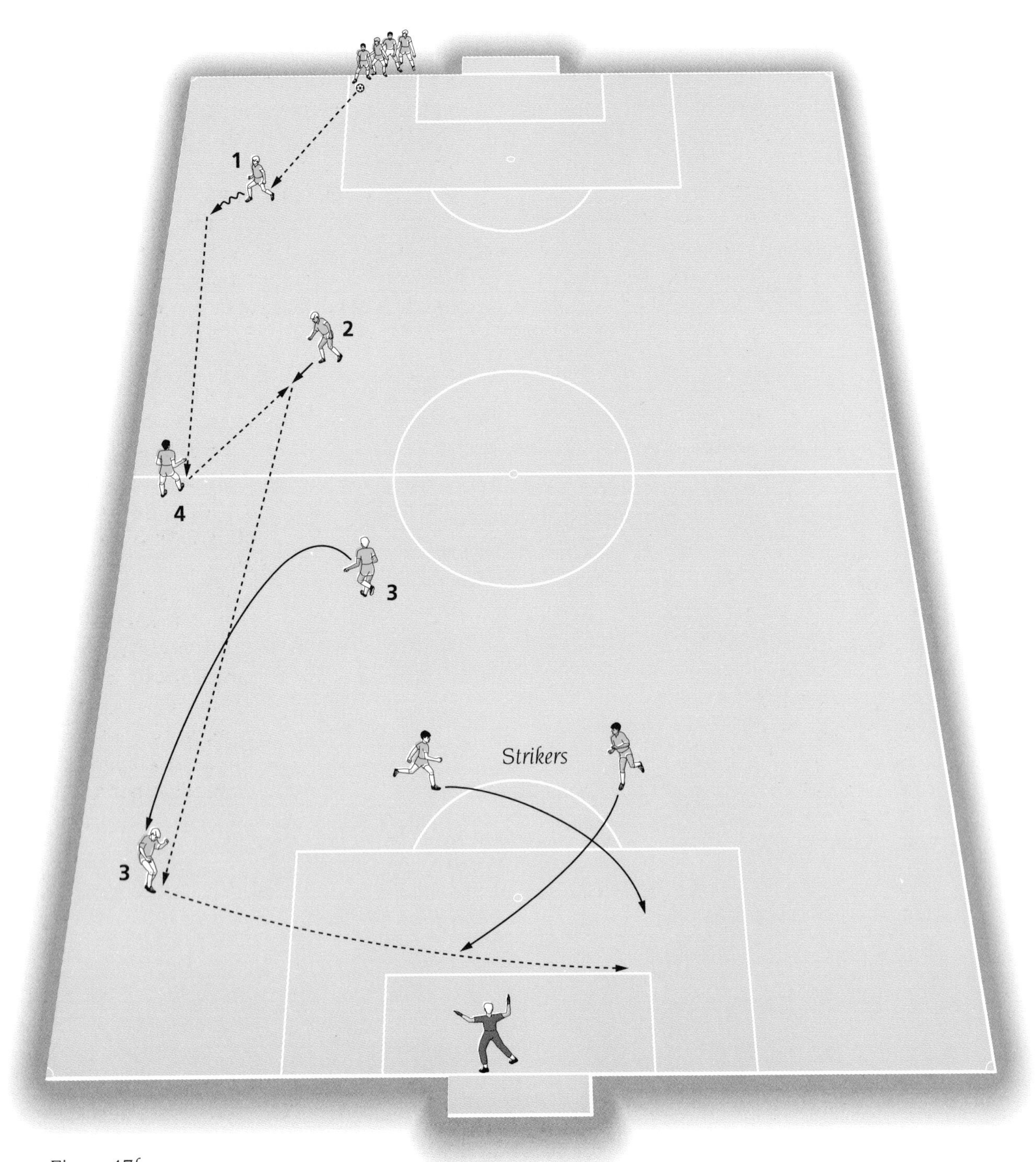

Figure 47b

Conclusion

Unopposed work prepares players to make 'third man' runs in a real game. A perceptive coach can cover all the technical points and put them to use in an opposed, small-sided game as preparation for the real thing. The movement in a three-against-three drill with support men (Figure 48) creates realistic situations (the grids are not essential). In this one, the players are coached to cross over, pass to feet and run beyond the ball if it has been set back, and to use the support players at both ends of the halfway line.

The coaching needs to remind the players to keep the shape of the team, and that the target is the fulcrum of attack. The coach also has to get his players to create movement. Sometimes it is worth stopping play to make a point, such as: 'If you had laid it in there and run forward, you could have created a "third man" movement yourself.'

The coach should also encourage diagonal runs, which present a greater danger to the defence than straight ones – in a match, the latter are more easily read by defenders and can take a player offside.

This three-against-three drill can eventually be extended to six against six on a pitch 65 yards in length. This will inevitably mean more runners, more defenders, more passing options and less space to attack. It will, in general, demand more patient passing and greater imagination with the through ball. Equally, defenders will recognize what the strikers are trying to do and will close down any space accordingly; attacking players will develop the ability to react to defenders and their moves. All this is good preparation for match play and an essential part of a young player's development.

Figure 48

IVECO
Ford

4
SETTING UP PLAY

A CRUCIAL PART OF attacking play is the setting up of a move with lay-offs, spins, twists and turns. By developing these skills on the training ground, players will be in a position to achieve greater penetration in match situations. Players who are comfortable playing and receiving balls with their back to goal, often under pressure from defenders, are crucial to any team. These drills should help you to develop this type of player.

Although training-ground drills at West Ham are often unopposed and without defenders, players have to develop skills that will allow them to combat the tight marking of match situations. The pass-and-move style of play requires players to be equipped to receive the ball under pressure and to make space even when tightly marked. These drills will help you prepare your players for the presence of defenders.

As explained earlier (see page 20), I coach players to stand in the half-turned position. First and foremost, a striker standing sideways on can see the defender behind him from the corner of his eye and, crucially, will be able to see if the defender drops off, giving him space to turn. This body position also allows players to receive the ball more efficiently and to act quickly.

The technical points to consider are that the receiver must have the ability to control or lay off the ball with his first touch; the ball is provided in the correct area for the receiver; both players – passer and receiver – know where the defender is; and the striker concentrates on the timing of his movement.

Opposite: *Setting the ball back. The player comes to meet the ball slightly on the half-turn and uses his back foot (here, the right) to set the ball back to his supporting players. Coming off on the half-turn gives the receiving player more options, which he can complete more easily than if he is standing square.*

Back-foot set-up

In this simple drill (Figure 49), two groups of four to six players stand behind two cones, 10 yards apart. Player 1, starting alongside and to the left of one of the cones, passes the ball with his right foot inside the opposite cone. Player 2, at the front of the opposite queue, moves to the left of his cone and lets the ball come on to his right (back) foot, playing it back to the spot where the first pass came from. This develops 'sideways running' away from the ball, with one foot coming across the other. The passer must always watch the path of the ball as he turns to join the back of his queue.

This sequence is repeated. The cones keep the distance between the two queues of players at approximately 10 yards and also ensure that each man comes off at an angle and avoids running straight at the ball to return the pass.

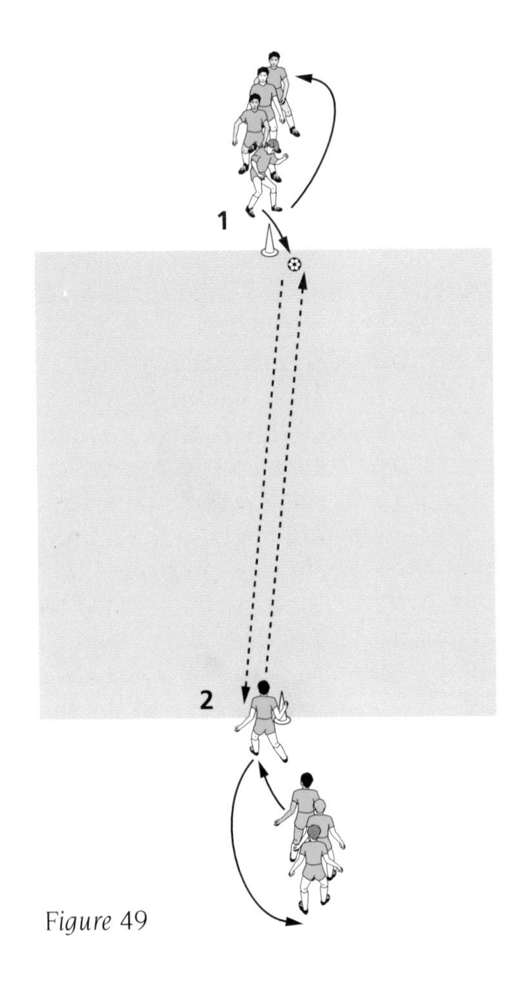

Figure 49

Back-foot passing

In this drill (Figure 50), the ball is not passed back in the same direction from which it came, and the players move in a third direction. Player 1, in the lower left-hand 'station' (corner) of the 10-yard square grid, passes to 4 and then runs forward, clockwise, towards 2. Player 4 plays the ball diagonally across the square to 2 and runs in a clockwise direction. Player 2, receiving from 4, plays the ball back from the top left station to the bottom left, to 5 (who is at 1's original station) and runs forward to 3's station. Player 5 passes the ball on the diagonal to 3, who is two stations further round.

In this drill, the players are reminded to 'Pass to where he's running'. The thought process can become muddled, so start the drill slowly! Ultimately, the six players should rotate continuously.

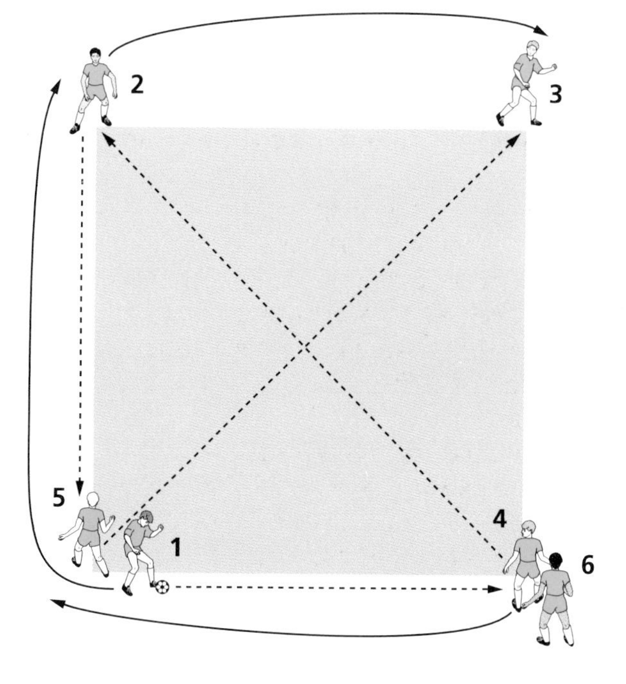

Figure 50

General set-up

In this drill (Figure 51), player 4 stands right on the edge of the penalty area. A queue of players stands 20 yards away from him, and two supporting players, 1 and 2, stand on either side, about 6 or 7 yards apart. Players 1 and 2 jog towards 3, the player with the ball at the head of the queue, who passes to 4 who is on the half-turn. As the ball is passed between them, players 1 and 2 turn and run goalwards, crossing over to support the target, 4. Player 4 can lay off the ball to 1 or 2 to shoot. Player 3 then swaps with 1 or 2, and 5 repeats the drill.

Set-up and crossing

In this variation on the previous drill (Figure 52), a wide player, 6, can receive the ball from 4, or from 1 if the ball is laid off to him. Players 1 and 2 make runs into the penalty box in anticipation of 6's cross.

Opposite: *Low, driven shot. As the player prepares to shoot, he is looking to drive the ball in to the far post. Note that his balance is good, his standing foot is placed nicely alongside the ball and the striking foot is poised to shoot, with the toe pointing down.*

Figure 51

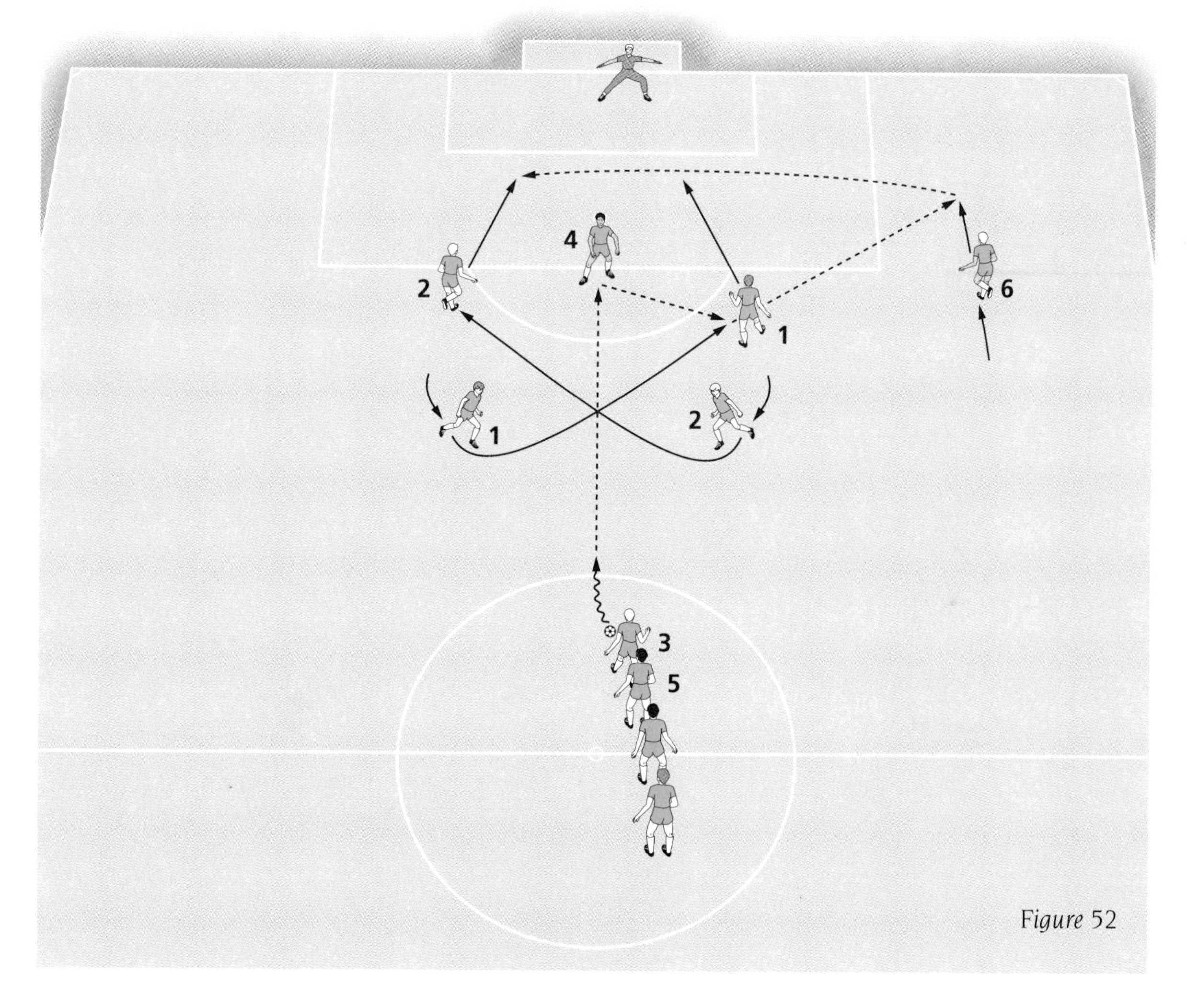

Figure 52

Spinning

In this drill (Figure 53), starting in the wide midfield area, player 2 passes the ball to the feet of the striker, 1, who in a match situation would have drawn the marking defender away from the penalty box (see the photograph opposite top). Player 1 lays the ball back to 2 (see the photograph opposite below) and then spins round on the outside of the defender – in this case, a cone – running right to left across the recovery line of the defender to gather 2's through ball, which is played inside the defender. Player 1 then shoots. Player 2 now becomes 1 and the drill is repeated. The playing of the ball up and back must be performed with pace, without losing the accuracy of the passing.

Figure 53

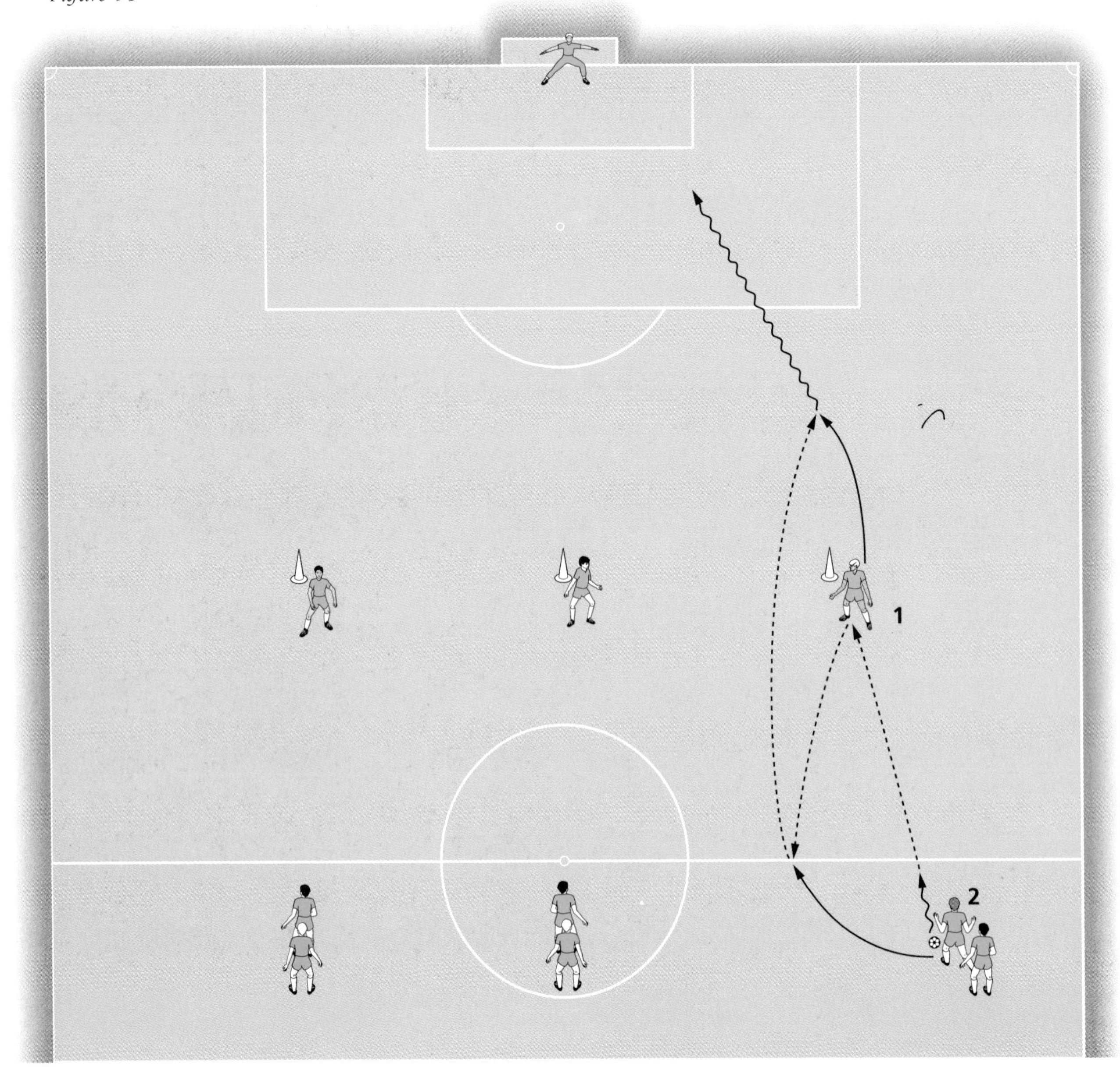

Player 2 looks to bring his forward towards the ball by pushing a pass into his feet.

Having brought his forward and the defender short, the player now looks to exploit the space behind the defender (see Figure 53).

Defence and midfield support

This drill (Figure 54) stretches play from one penalty area to the other. The goalkeeper serves the ball from the 6-yard box to one of his defenders: the left-back 3, the centre-back 2, or the right full-back 1. Receiving on the half-turn, the player, in this case 1, can now pass to any one of the three midfield players, 4, 5 or 6.

If the ball is laid up to the right midfield player, 4, who then returns it, the right-back has the option of hitting any of the three targets – with a straight ball to 7, an angled ball to 8, or a diagonal ball to 9. In this example, he passes to 7, who then finds 4, who has turned and can now shoot.

There are numerous variations on this drill and the coach can dictate a particular theme or, after a while, let the players make the decisions on varying the drill.

Figure 54

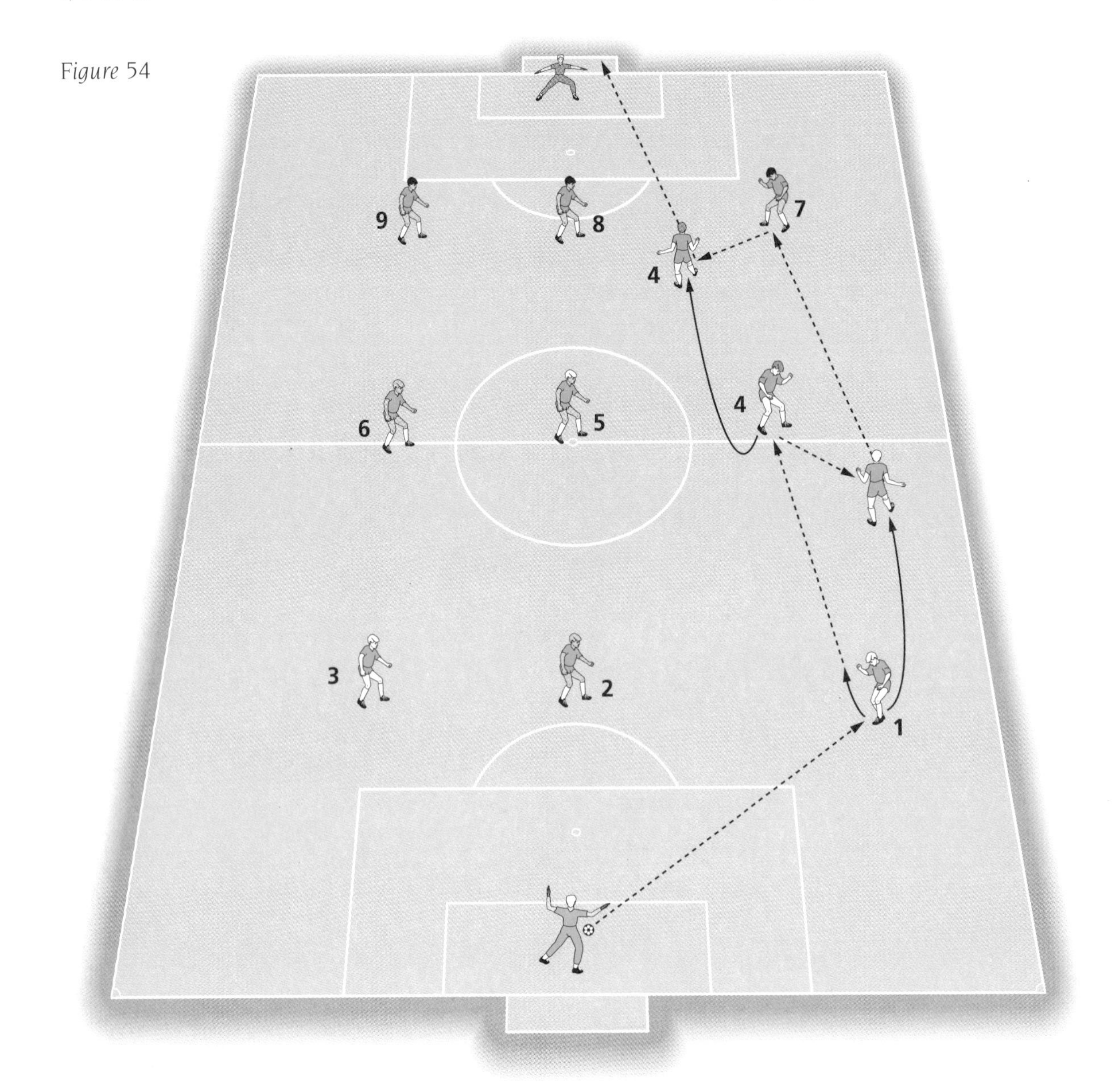

Complex spinning

In this drill (Figure 55a), player 3 has the ball. A striker, 1, moves to draw his defender with him, and when 3 chooses to pass to his partner 2, 1 spins away to give 2 a passing option.

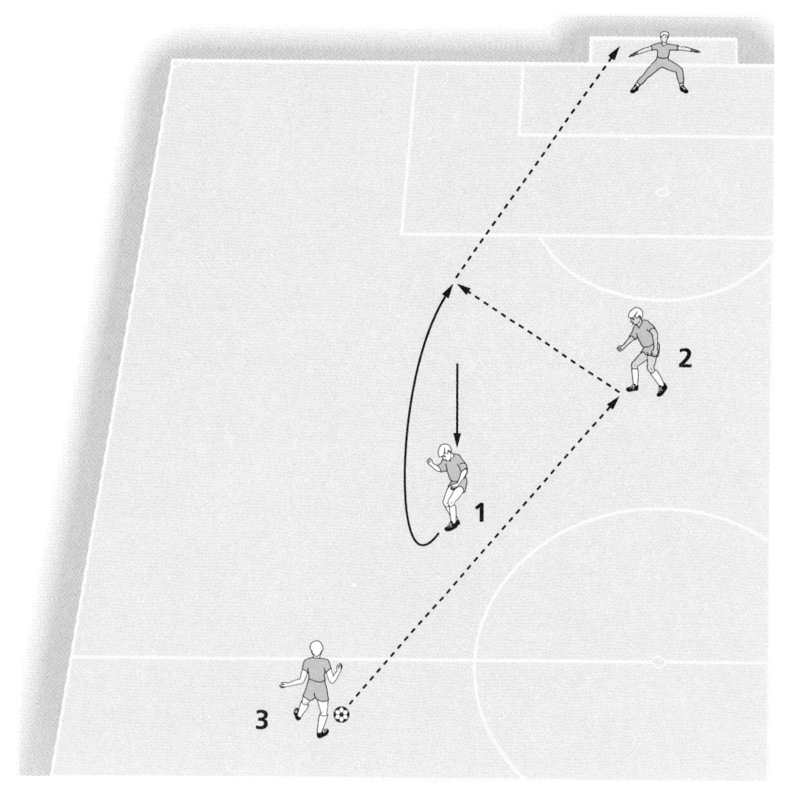

Figure 55a

In a variation of this drill (Figure 55b), player 3 finds 2. Player 1 has spun and come across in front of 2, who passes to him before himself spinning and running for a return and perhaps also a shot at goal.

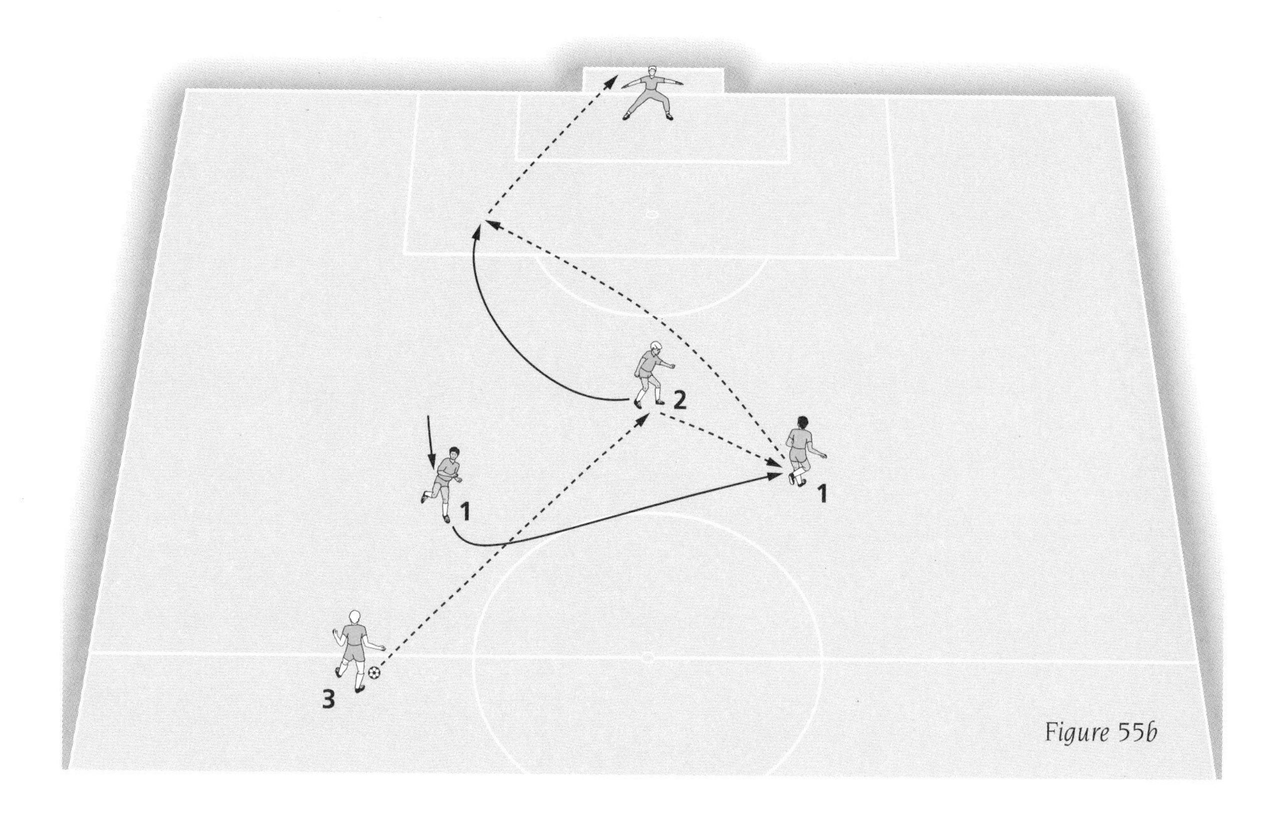

Figure 55b

In Figure 55c, player 1 comes short to make space behind himself and then spins to slip on to the through ball from 2 down the wide channel. Having received the ball from player 2, 1 then cuts back the ball for 2 – who has run into the penalty box – to shoot.

Figure 55c

In Figure 55d, player 1 moves towards 3, who passes so that he can turn with the ball. He then finds the cross-field run of 2. Timing of the run and pass is crucial, with offside being a factor.

It is up to individual players to recognize situations as they arise in a match and pick the best option from these four, which are all common match scenarios. Through coaching, prompting and discussion, players will learn to choose the correct passes and movements during matches.

Figure 55d

Dummy, spin and shoot

In this drill (Figure 56), player 1 moves to receive the ball from a queue of servers at a wide angle. The ball is played slightly to one side and player 1 dummies to play it, before spinning round and letting it run on to 2, who in return lays it off to 1, who has continued his run and then shoots.

To repeat this drill, the original wide-angle server becomes player 2, and 2 becomes 1. The drill can be alternated down either wing.

Figure 56

Cross-over

In this drill (Figure 57), player 1 passes square to his partner, 2, who lays the ball up to the first striker, 3, while the second striker, 4, makes a cross-over run behind 3 into space down the right. Player 3 lays off the ball to 2 and spins to take up the opposite attacking position to 4. Player 2 can then pass to either 4 or 3. To repeat the drill, players 1 and 2 become 3 and 4.

Figure 57

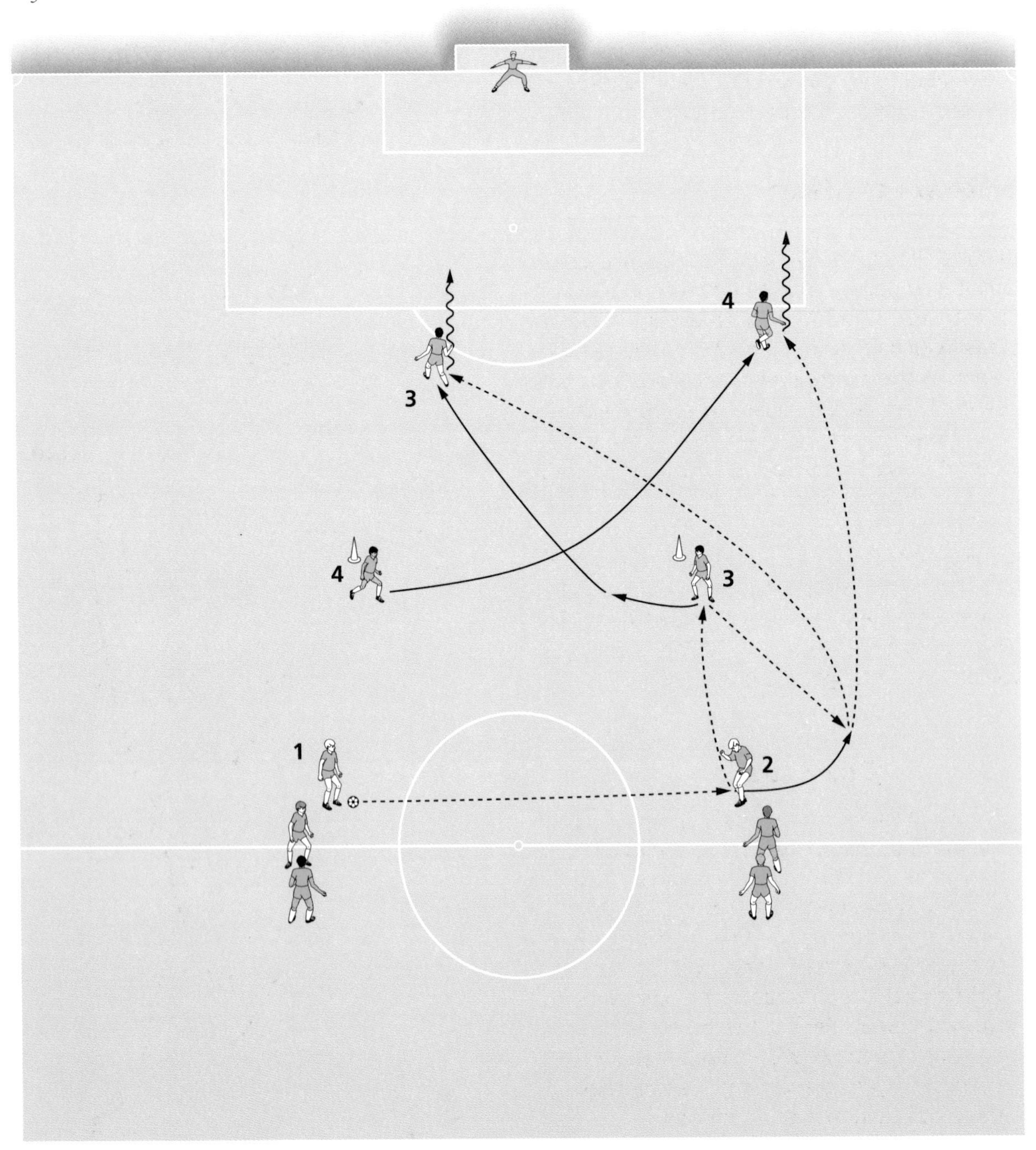

Interpassing

This drill (Figure 58), using two stacked 10-yard square grids, is basic setting-up play. Player 1 passes to 2, who has moved away from his 'marking' cone. Player 2 sets the ball back to 1, who has followed his pass and transfers the ball through to 3, waiting in a queue at the other end. Player 1 then joins 3's queue, while 3 passes first time to 4, and they then repeat the pattern of 1 and 2, with 3 finally joining 1's original queue.

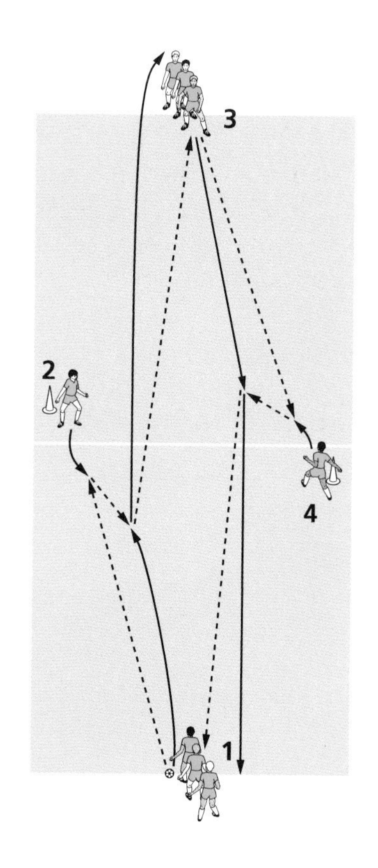

Figure 58

Set-up rotation

In this drill (Figure 59) – which is a bit like a ball circuit (see page 102) in that it is continuous – team-mates 3 and 4 work as a pair. Player 1 starts with the ball in the bottom left-hand corner of the marked-out area (grids are not essential) and lays it square to 2, following his pass. Player 3 comes towards 2 at an angle. Player 4, more central, receives the ball from 2 and then finds 3, who has turned to take the pass. Player 3 then passes to 6 in the corner and follows the path of his pass, while 6 squares the ball to 5. To repeat, 2 takes 3's place in the centre, a new player takes over 1's berth, and the direction is reversed, 4 now being the player going short to support 6's pass to 5.

Figure 59

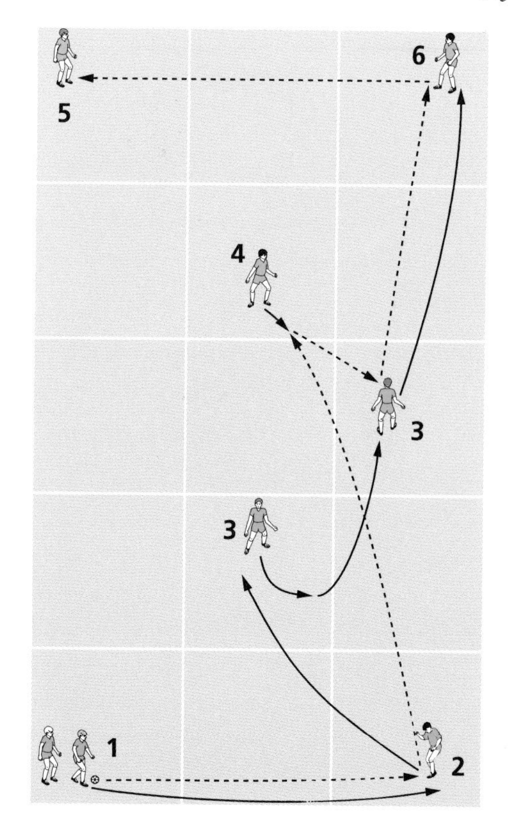

Conclusion

Unopposed drills allow young players the opportunity to refine their technique. The drills covered in this chapter will prepare your players for the discipline of playing against opposition and coping with being marked, and will develop habits that are conducive to pass-and-move football. Perfect the drills so that setting up play will become second nature and the players will be ready for the pressure of match situations.

IVECO
DAGENHAM MOTORS
DAGENHAM MOTORS

5 WALL PASSING

THE WALL PASS – where one player acts as a 'wall' for a pass from a team-mate – is an effective tactic for getting in behind even the tightest of modern defences. The strength of the 'one-two', as it is also known, is based on running at space, at speed. Perfecting the drills will help to improve a player's capacity for defensive penetration.

Wall pass

This drill (Figure 60) uses three cones as defenders, spread across the top of the penalty area. Player 1, approximately 10 yards away from the central cone, runs towards the highlighted space, at pace, controlling the ball with the outside of his front foot (in a match, he would be trying to commit the defender). The wall passer, 2, beside the cone, stands in a half-turned position and player 1 fires in the ball to his right (back) foot to play a one-two with him. Player 1 receives a return pass and finishes with a shot, preferably, but not essentially, first time.

The other two cones can be used to give different angles of attack. You must try to get your players to perform the practice with as much pace as their ability allows.

Figure 60

The wall pass. Player 2 runs with the ball towards the defender.

Player 2 passes the ball in to his team-mate to his right and carries his run forward into the penalty area.

The receiving player uses his right foot as a rebound surface and guides the return pass behind the committed defender. It is important that the player puts the correct amount of pace on the ball, so that the return ball is left playable for the oncoming forward.

One wall

This drill (Figure 61) incorporates close control and moving the ball quickly around the defender with the wall on the half-turn. A constant wall (5) operates in the two stacked 10-yard square grids, while the pairs of players at each end (1 and 2, 3 and 4) continually reverse their roles.

In the top square, player 1 has the ball and 2 is a notional defender. Player 1 lays the ball to the constant wall (5) and receives the ball back on the run. He passes directly up to the other end. Player 3 receives the ball and moves to attack 4, who, like 2, is acting as a passive defender. Meanwhile, the constant wall (5) has run diagonally across into the bottom square and is available for 3 to use as a wall. A left-sided wall can also be used. The constant wall can be either on the left or the right of the grid.

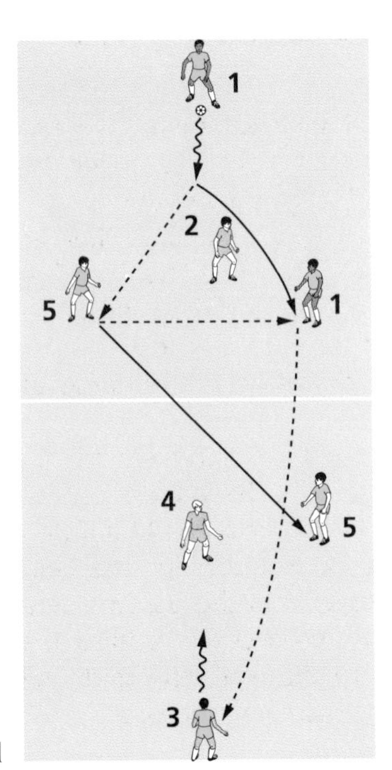

Figure 61

Figure 62

Rotational wall pass

This drill (Figure 62) equates to a match situation where a winger is receiving the ball from distance. The ball is arriving at waist or knee height, so the winger plays the ball inside – on the volley or with a cushioned header – to his supporting midfield player, and runs down the side of the four stacked 10-yard square grids, using the midfield player as a wall.

Player 1 in the bottom square has the ball, 2 is the passive defender and 3 is the wall. Player 1 draws 2 towards him and then plays a one-two off 3 and chips the ball to 4, the winger. Player 5 is the passive defender and lets the ball go over his head to 4, allowing 4 to volley to his wall, the midfielder 6. The exercise can then be repeated.

Wall-pass combination

This drill (Figure 63) shows how the wall pass can open up the game. Player 1 passes between two cones to 2 and makes a run to one side. Player 2, a midfielder, returns the ball – acting as a wall. Player 1 can now find the movement of 3, who in turn can find 2, who has swivelled and turned to make himself free after making his pass and can now dribble and shoot. To repeat, player 1 becomes 2, 2 becomes 3 and 3 goes back to the queue.

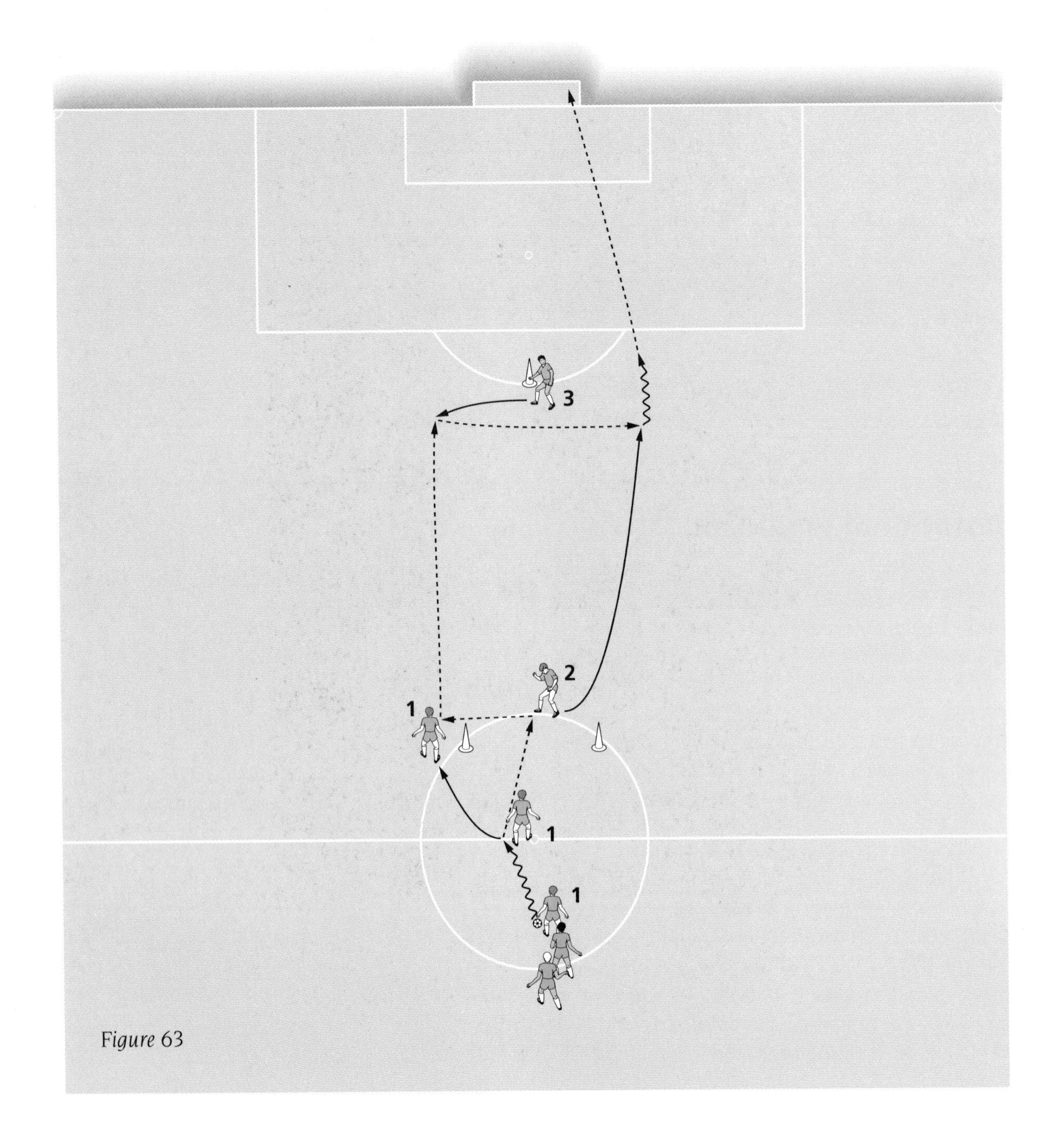

Figure 63

Conclusion

A good wall pass can be very effective, and once it has been mastered your players will have a very effective attacking weapon. A great many players fail to differentiate between the first ball played into the wall, which should have 'pace', and lay-offs, which require the pace to be taken off the ball so as to leave it playable. Coach these distinctions into your players and they will be able to perfect their wall passing and benefit from it in matches.

David Platt, an attacking midfield player, provides a perfect example of the effectiveness of the wall pass. He is a player who always picks the ball up just outside the penalty area, and looks to play off his team-mates in wall-pass fashion to get himself behind the defence and into scoring positions.

SOUTH EASTERN
ELECTRICAL PLC
081-
506 1717
LONGLIFE ROOFING
TEL:0171-537 3713
PONY
PONY
LJK
FOR SALES SERVICE BODYSHOP
AND PARTS CALL 0181-500 1090
A Night You'll Remember
CORAL
ROMFORD STADIUM
Greyhound Racing
NORTHERN
4

6 CROSSING

GOOD CROSSING EXPLOITS good possession in dangerous wide positions to the full. Time spent practising crossing will ensure that good possession in attacking situations is less likely to be wasted.

Selecting which type of cross is required depends on the individual player recognizing the situation confronting him in the penalty area. The four zones I consider to be vulnerable goal-scoring areas (Figure 64) are the near-post zone, 1, which is the area just before and just beyond the near post; the central zone, 2, which is the area between the posts; the far-post zone, 3, which is at and beyond the far post; and the cut-back zone, 4, which is the area around the penalty spot and out to the edge of the box.

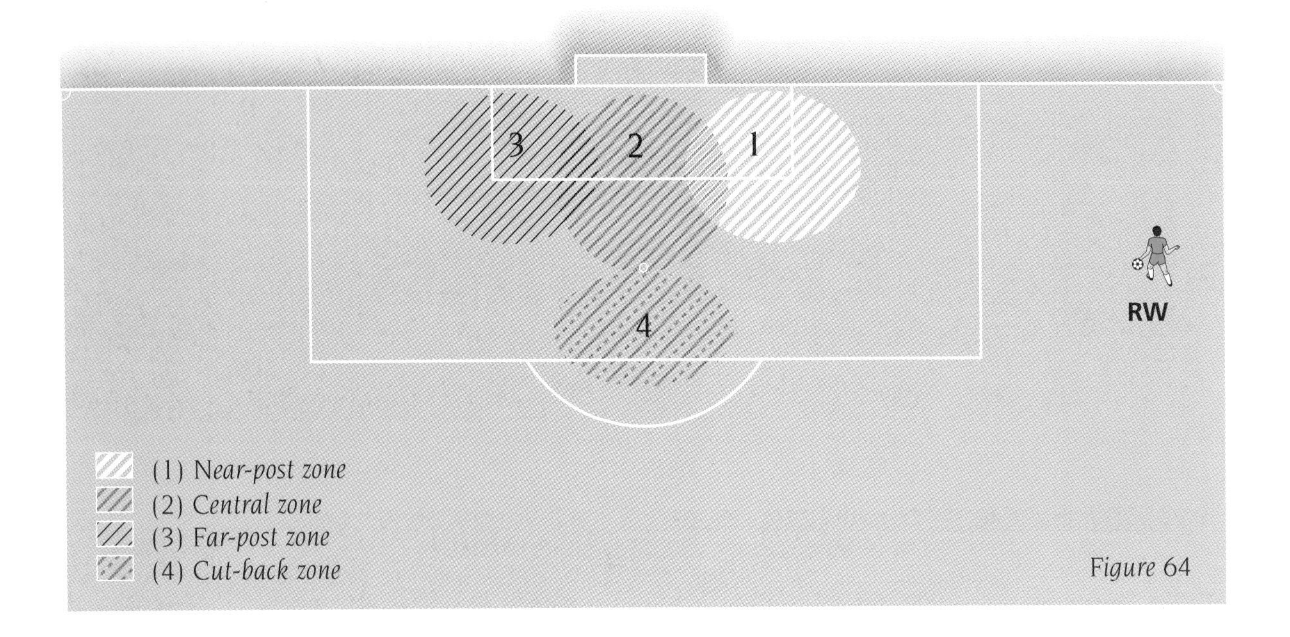

Figure 64

Which cross is most appropriate depends on how spread out the defence is, how much space there is, and where the strikers are positioned: there are no hard-and-fast rules. The ball has to be put into the box as accurately as possible, and each situation presents different problems for the wide player as he is about to cross the ball. The crosser will have to consider whether to put the cross into the near post; curl or bend the

Chipped cross. The player makes contact with the ball with his toe underneath it. His body is leaning away, emphasizing the need to chip the ball over the defender.

Cut-back from the goal-line. The player in possession arrives at the goal-line and prepares to cross the ball.

Note that all the defenders are drawn towards the near post, and the crosser cuts the ball back towards the penalty spot for the player just arriving in the box.

The player arriving late attacks the ball and looks to shoot. The space has been created by the crosser, who has drawn the defence towards the goal before cutting back the ball.

cross around a defender; chip the ball up over the defenders to the back post; cut the ball back for a striker's late run; or drive the cross in quickly behind the defenders and in front of the goalkeeper. Against a retreating defence, all the wide player may need to do is put the ball across the face of the goal behind the retreating defenders and hope that one of his front men will be on the end of it. This crossed ball will often need reasonable pace.

One of the most common faults when crossing a ball is the inability to cut out the defender at the near post. By putting yourself, or a spare player, there as a dummy defender on the training ground you can drill your players in how to avoid having their crosses cut out.

Low, driven cross. With the defence retreating, the player looks to drive the ball low across the penalty area. Note that his body and head are down over the ball.

On contact, the player's head stays down and he drives the ball in to the space between the defenders and goalkeeper.

Near-post cross

This drill (Figure 65) can be alternated from either wing. Player 1 takes the ball wide of the target cone – or a very passive defender – and curls, bends, chips or pushes it into the highlighted space between the post and the edge of the 6-yard box. Player 2, who starts behind a cone, attacks the near post.

The ball must be crossed into the space and not at the attacking player. Player 2 must run at the area at which the ball is being aimed, which usually requires him to make an early run to get in front of the goalkeeper and across defenders. (see the photograph on page 64).

Figure 65

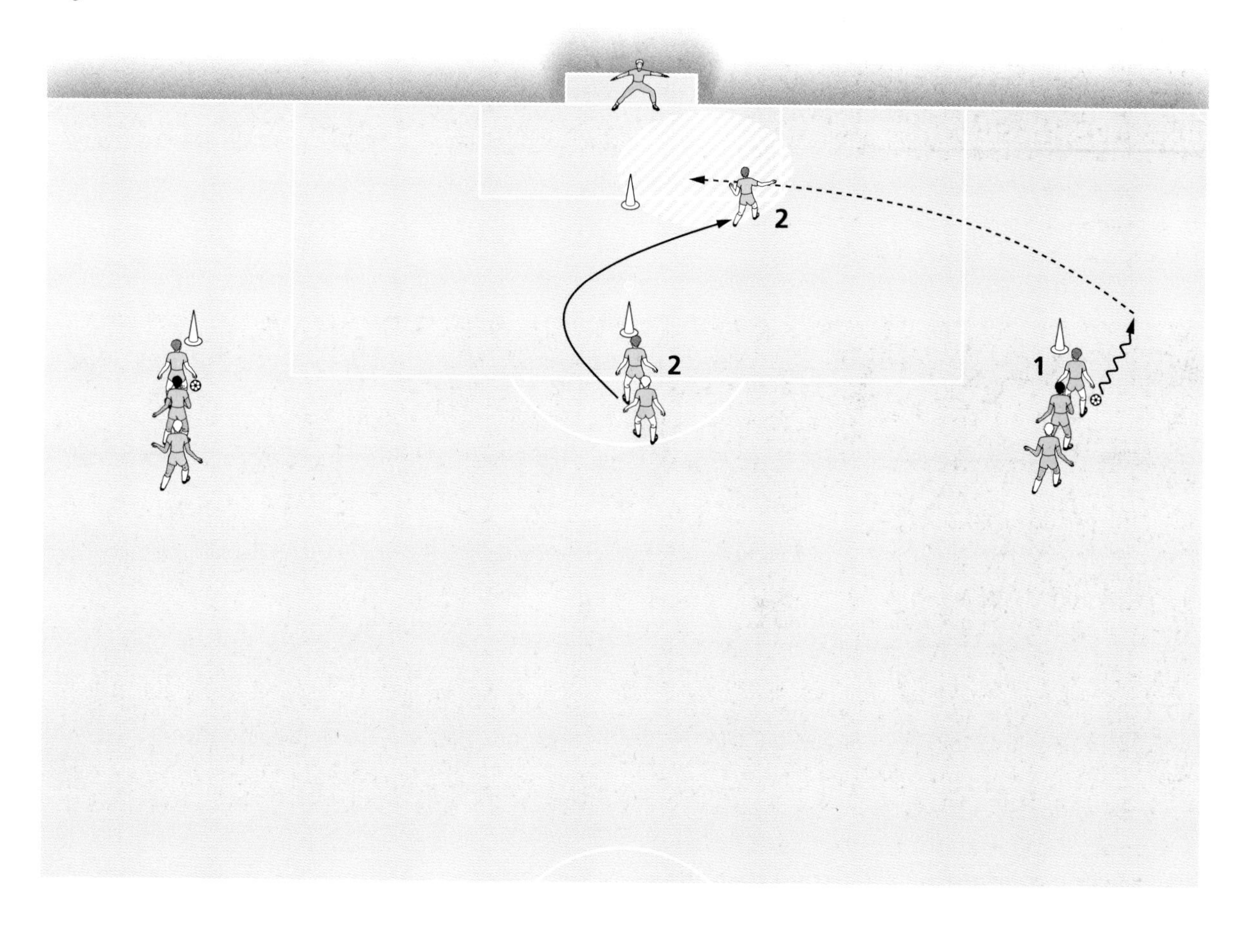

Near-post set-up

This drill (Figure 66) can be alternated from either wing. Player 1 passes to 2, who has moved in front of the cone and returns the ball to 1's feet. Player 1 crosses the ball to player 3, who has run between the cones to the near post.

Figure 66

Set-up overlap

This drill (Figure 67) can be alternated from either wing. Players 5 and 6 are positioned in the outside-left area, round about the top corner of the penalty box. Two strikers, 1 and 2, stand 10 yards outside the edge of the box.

Player 3 starts the move by passing to 4 and making an easy angle. Player 4 returns the pass to 3, who finds the nearer wide player, 5. Player 6 makes an overlapping run around the back of 5, who feeds him the ball to cross into the box. Meanwhile, players 1 and 2 make runs to the far and near post respectively for one of the pair to score.

Timing-wise, when player 6 draws his leg back to cross, 2 should be inside the box and

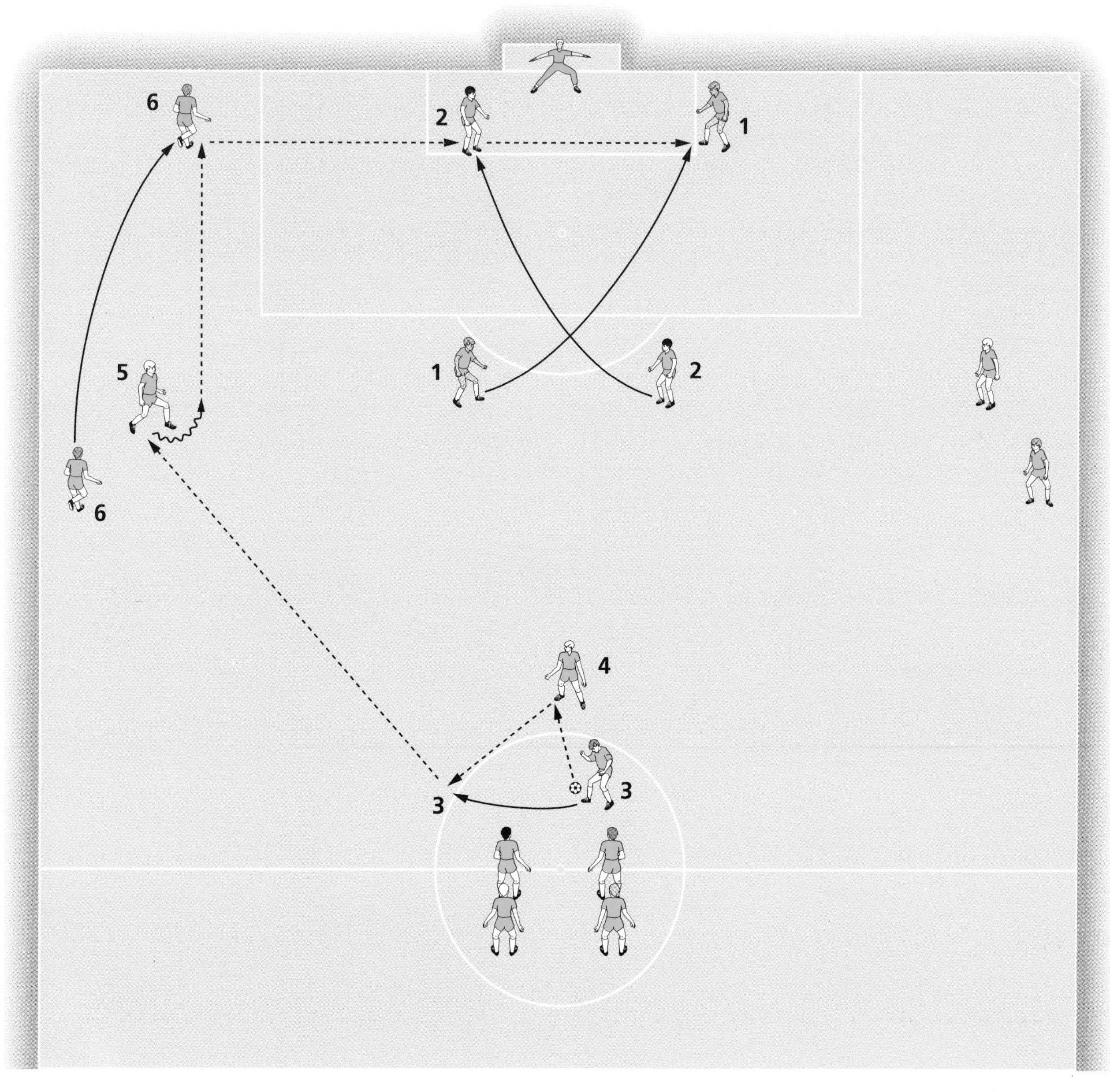

Figure 67

ready to attack the space on the near post. Player 1 at the far post should aim to leave as much space as possible in front of him, so that he is not caught jumping from a standing position and can attack the ball that may have eluded 2. The accuracy of the cross is crucial to any crossing exercise. Common faults include not by-passing the defender on the near post or not looking up to see what the forwards are doing prior to crossing. Constant practice is the key and, through trial and error, the wide players and strikers will develop a good understanding of crossing and goal-scoring opportunities will be created.

Three against two in the box

The onus is on the wide players in this drill. Once they are in a position on the goal-line, they must decide which crossing technique to use. Do they push the ball into the near post? Cut it back to the penalty spot area? Chip it up to the far post, or drill it across the 6-yard box? There are many options and the choice will be dictated by the positions of the defenders and the runs of the attackers.

The drill (Figure 68a) starts with 5 setting the ball up off 1 (who is marked) and then passing to wide player 3. As 3 controls and starts to run with the ball to the goal-line, attackers 1, 2 and 5 make runs into the box, anticipating the cross. The two defenders must track the runs of the attackers.

In Figure 68b player 3 is on the goal-line with the ball, 2 has made a run to the near post, 1 has pulled away to the far post and 5 is arriving in the box late in a central position. The wide player 3 decides to cut the ball back to 5, as the two defenders have been drawn towards the goal. The defenders must attempt to stop a goal being scored as the attackers try to take intelligent positions to lose the defenders. After three or four attacks the two defenders change with a resting pair; the attackers change after every attack, and alternate right and left sides.

Figure 68a

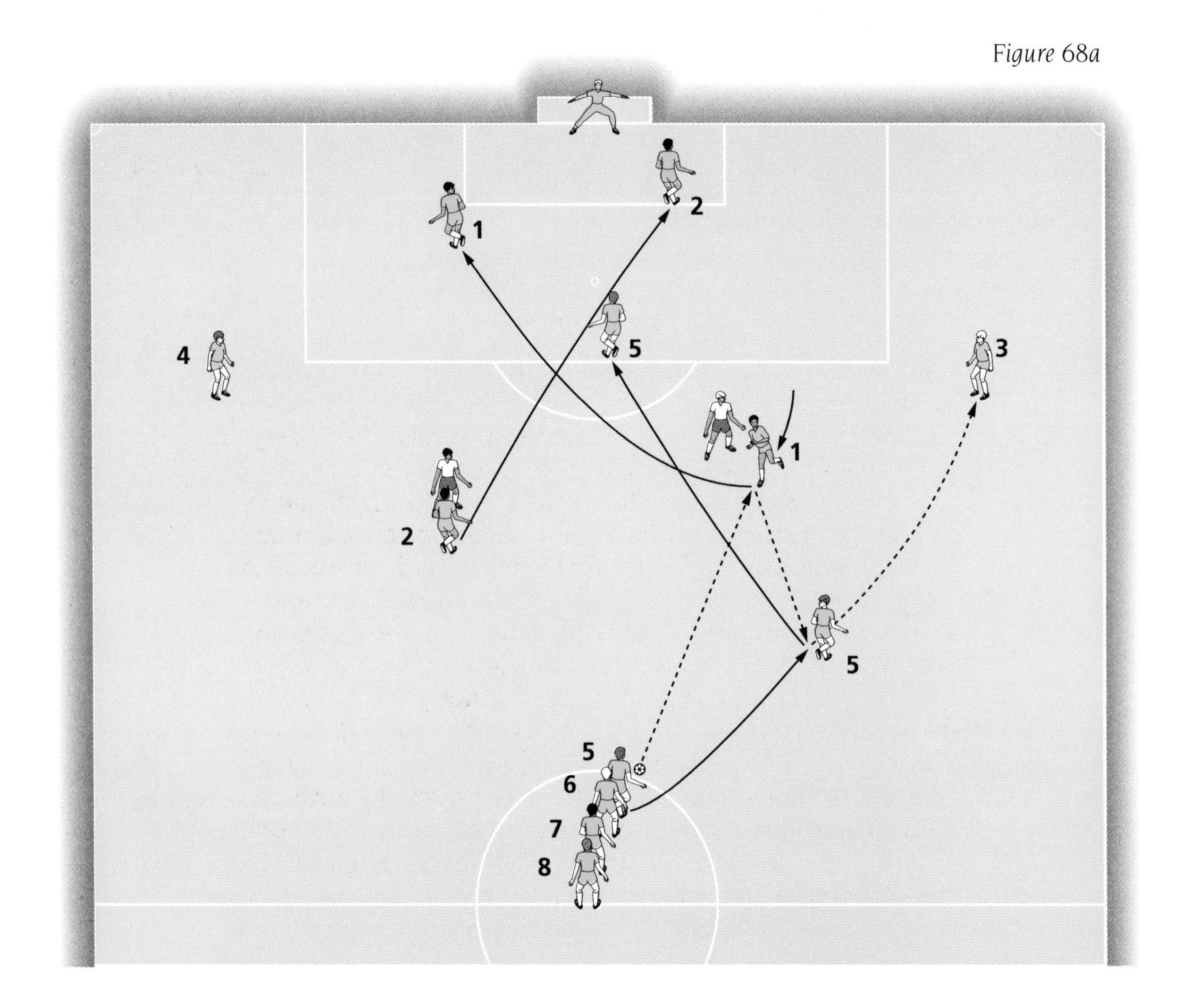

Figure 68b

Conclusion

When a ball is crossed, it's up to the determination of the attackers to put themselves to the ball. There is rarely a 'free' (unchallenged) header or shot, so it is important to encourage young players to attack the ball and not wait for it.

If the ball is at head or chest height the attacker should try to make good contact with his head and aim for one of the corners of the goal. If the ball is whipped in with pace around waist height, you will be looking for the attacker to make at least enough contact to guide the ball on target – even the faintest of touches can be enough to put the ball in the back of the net. The cross may also be drilled along the ground, in which case general shooting techniques apply. Tell your players: 'Hit the target, you can't always be technically correct.'

Adjustment and improvisation are key assets in situations close to goal. Sometimes the players must simply try to make the best of the delivery into the box. We seek perfection, but in reality we often do not get it!

CARLING
PREMIERSHIP

7
DEFENDING

UNOPPOSED DRILLS ALLOW players to develop attacking skills and the pass-and-move game, but at some point the coach must turn his attention to defending. Determination, bravery, strength and pace, together with good technical ability, are qualities that should be looked for in young defenders.

Different situations will make different demands on defenders and it is not always possible for them to be calm and in control of every situation, but, basically, defending is about being first to the ball and preventing goal-scoring opportunities. Of course, if defenders can break up attacks and keep good control of the ball, then the defenders themselves become the first line of attack for their team.

The drills in this chapter should instil the basic principles of defending in your players.

THE BASICS OF JOCKEYING

Jockeying – pressurizing the player with the ball – is a key part of defending and a discipline at which West Ham left- and right-backs Frank Lampard and Billy Bonds were masters. It involves getting as close to the player with the ball as possible, to be within tackling distance (about 1 yard), thereby delaying and manipulating the attack.

The defender must get low, slightly half-turned, and stay balanced on his toes, with bodyweight evenly distributed between both feet so that the player can edge closer to the ball and have the option of tackling when absolutely sure of winning the ball. Whether the defender shows the attacker in-field or down the line is a matter of personal choice for the coach.

Jockeying: showing in-field. The defender takes up a position angling the forward inside and into the covering player.

As the forward moves with the ball, the defender edges closer, making sure he does not allow the forward to check back and go down the line. He wants the forward to come in-field, where he has cover and play may be congested.

Jockeying: showing down the line. The angle of approach for the defender (6) shows the forward the space down the line.

The defender has now turned and is closing in on the running forward. The covering player (7) is poised to help if the forward over-runs the ball or the defender is outrun.

One against one

In this drill (Figure 69), which takes place within two stacked 10-yard square grids, the defender, O, lays the ball into the attacker's square and then moves to shut him down. The attacker, 1, has to get the ball into the defender's square before he can score in the goal at the far end of the defender's square, and is not allowed to bend the ball around him. The players can, of course, swap roles.

The defender should aim to be close enough to 'threaten the ball' and also block off the attacker. He can use his arms to make himself look bigger, and his stance should allow him good turning angles and prevent him being caught on the front foot.

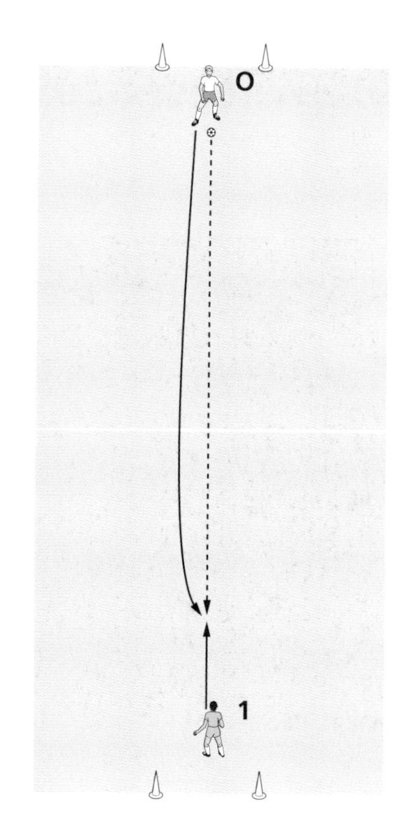

Figure 69

One-against-one halves

In this drill (Figure 70) there are two goalkeepers, two pairs of defenders and attackers, and four support players lining the two-grid area (which was positioned on the pitch as shown when I staged the drill, although this is not essential). Using his defender teammate and support players, an attacker, 1, has to find his opponents' goalkeeper with a pass. After a 'goal', the defender is allowed the first touch in the reverse play, before the attacker facing him is allowed to close him down.

The defensive techniques to coach are getting as close to the attacker as possible and preventing him turning; denying the attacker space to run if he has already turned; tracking the attacker's run and staying between him and the goal; protecting the space behind when the ball is laid out to the outside supporting player.

Encourage bright attacking play: it requires the defensive players to respond adequately and be just as bright. If you can, I recommend using the top strikers at your club against young defenders to test their ability to think and react quickly. The better the forward play the better the defending has to be.

Figure 70

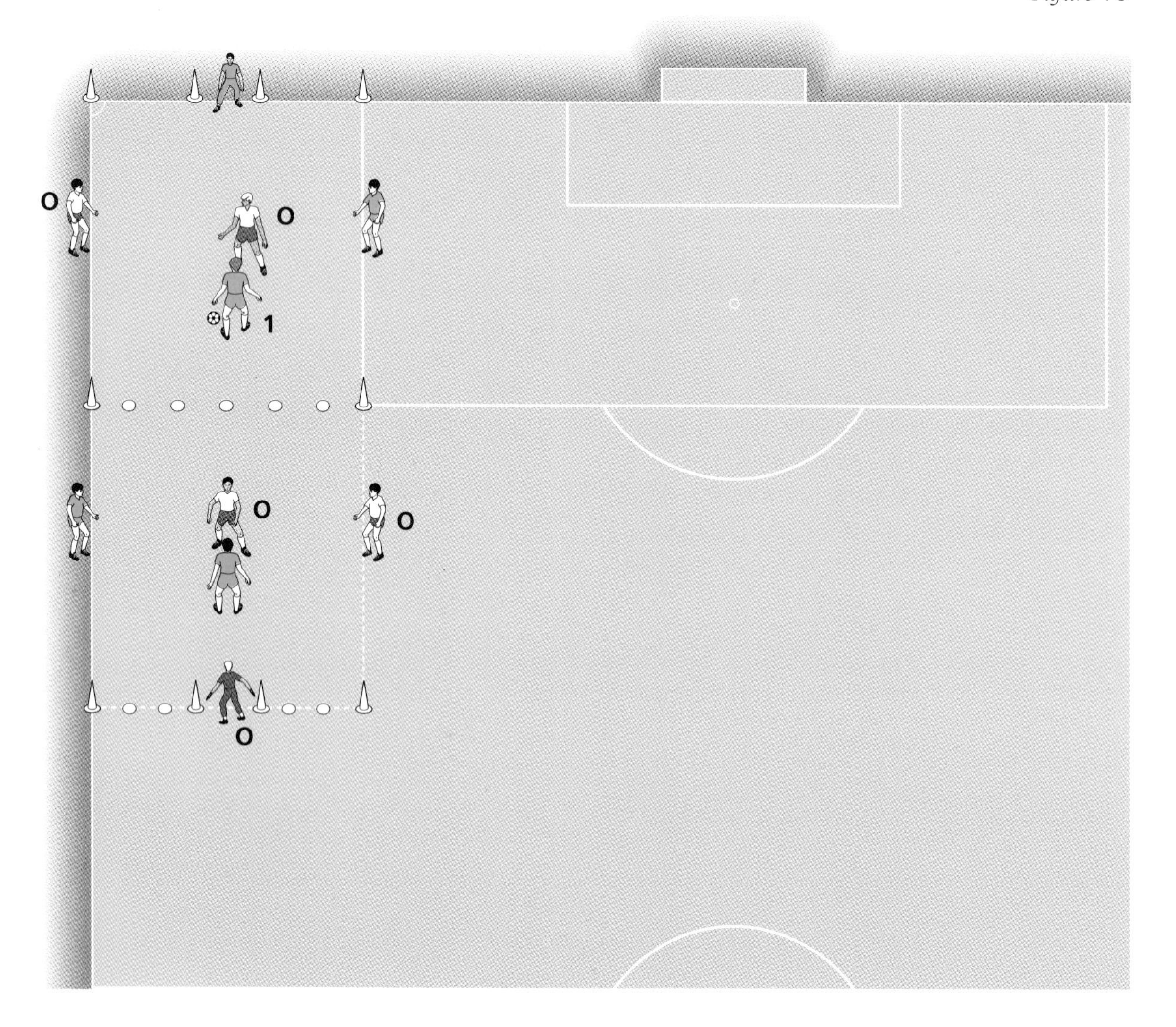

Two against two

Many aspects of defending can be highlighted in this drill (Figure 71), practised in six 10-yard square grids stacked as shown, with a target player at one end for the attackers and a server at the other to start the exercise. The defenders, O1 and O2, try to deny the attackers space and prevent them from 'scoring' by passing to the goalkeeper, and success to the defenders is winning possession or forcing it out of play. You can introduce support players to aid the attackers and give the defenders more problems.

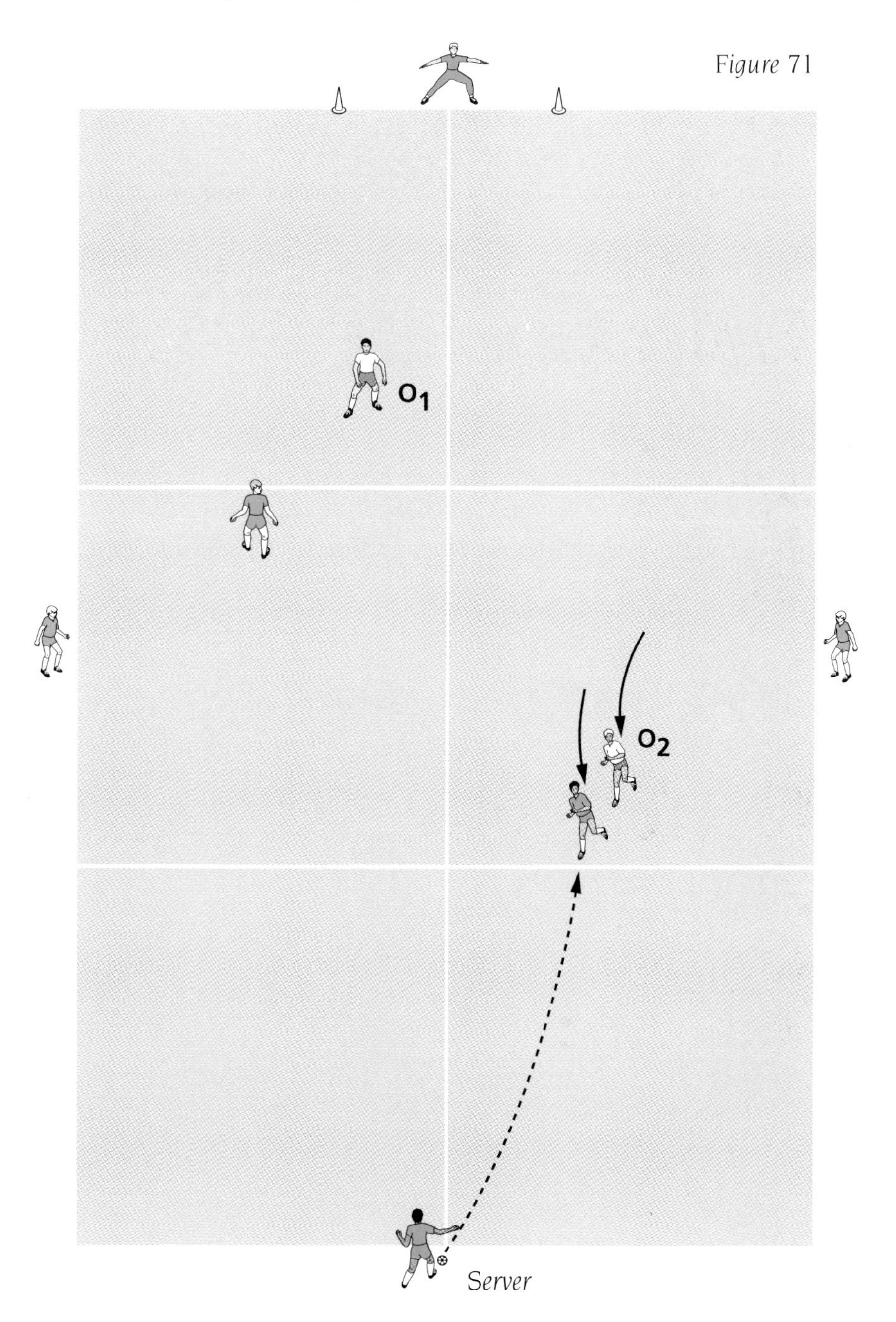

Figure 71

Five against three

In defending, it is as just as important to ask yourself, 'How hard are the players working to win the ball back?' The aim of this drill (Figure 72) is to pressurize and regain possession.

The three defenders (O1, O2 and O3) are outnumbered by five attackers in an area made up of four 10-yard square grids arranged in a block as shown. Initially, the practice allows a maximum of two touches. The defensive objective is to dispossess the attackers (1, 2, 3, 4 and 5) five times.

The first player, O1, closes down 2, thereby shutting off the passing angle to 1 and making it 'four against three'. Defender O1 tries to make 2 delay his pass, because the more he delays the more closely the defender can pressure the ball. Defenders O2 and O3 must block off 2's route to 5 (in the middle) and 4 (in the diagonally opposite corner), and also pressure the square pass from 2 to 3.

The defenders are making the attackers play into areas which are as small as possible so that they can intercept, tackle the player as he receives the ball, or force an error in his control so that the ball passes out of play.

On hearing information from his back-up support of O2 and O3, O1 must move quickly to close down 2. Between them, they must shut off the angled pass, delay and force a controlling touch in order to prevent 2 playing the ball first time, and make 2 play square to 3.

This drill equates to a match situation where your challenging midfield player shuts off the opposing midfield player's forward passing options and forces him to go square or lay the ball backwards. If winning the ball becomes too easy, take out a defender, or keep the same numbers and enlarge the playing area, making it easier to keep possession, or remove the two-touch restriction.

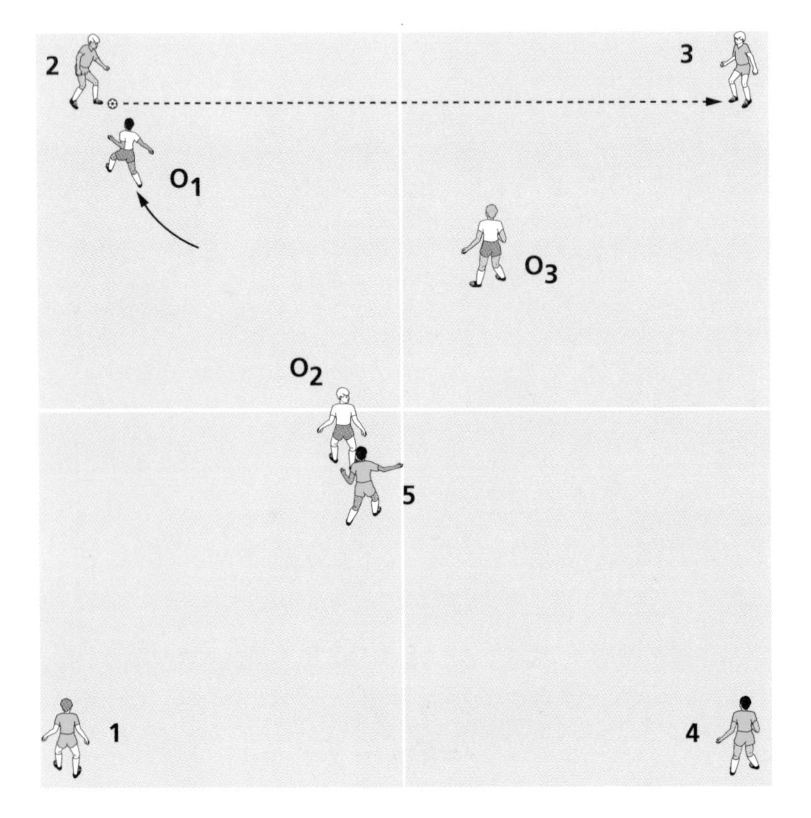

Figure 72

Three against three

Using a mobile goal and the pitch marked out as shown (Figure 73), you can now build up the practice to match-like situations, in and around the penalty area. Here there are three defenders working three forwards in each half of the marked area. There are also four 'wingers', one right and one left in each half. Their job is to cross the ball as early as possible for their forwards, who try to score. The defenders must try to prevent the forwards shooting directly at goal, and if the ball goes wide they will defend the cross as they would have to in a game.

Figure 73

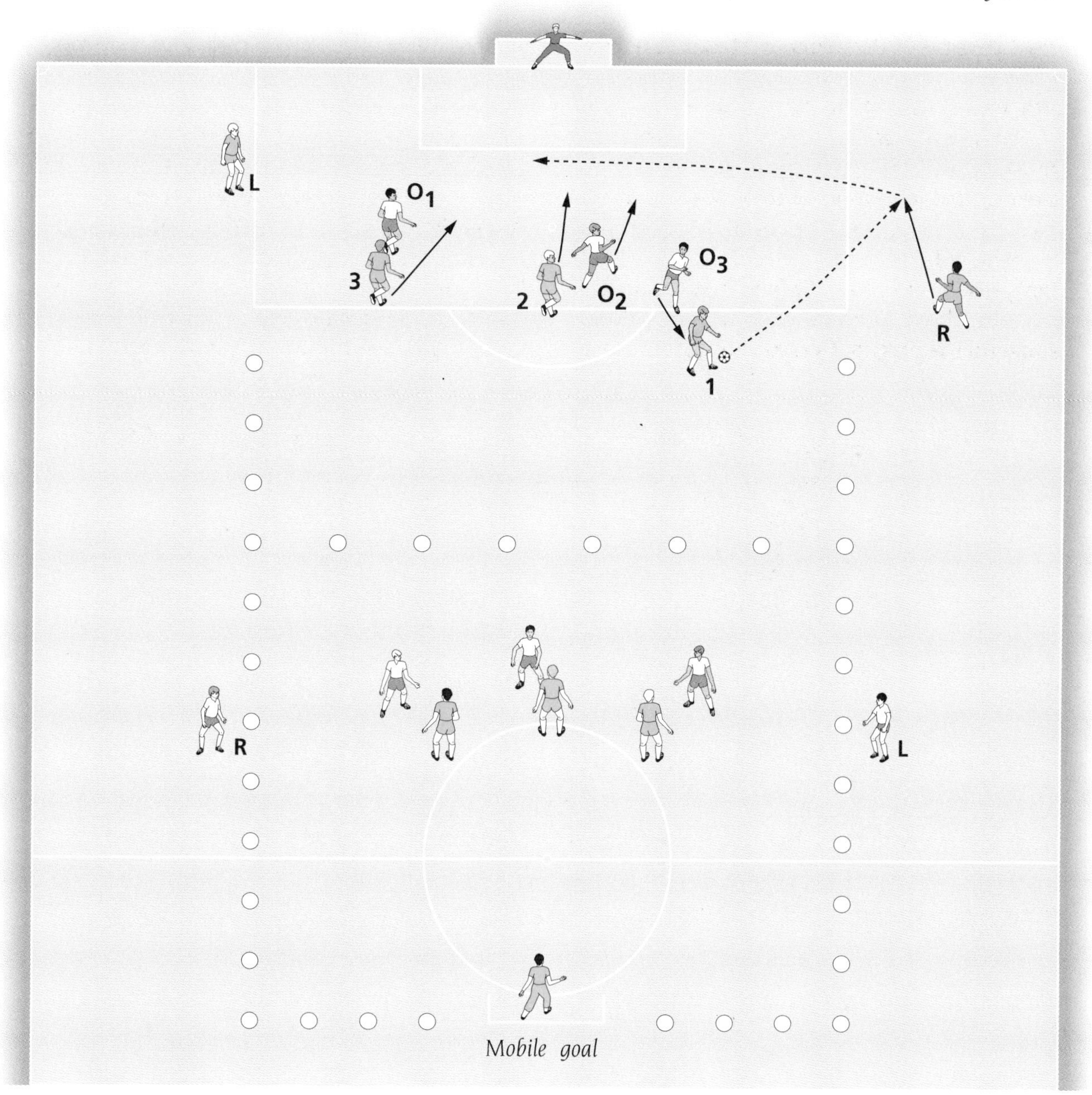

In Figure 73, 1 has the ball and cannot shoot directly at goal because the defender O3 has closed off his space. Player 1 elects to pass the ball wide to his winger R, who crosses the ball in for forwards 2 and 3. It is now up to defenders O1 and O2 to defend the cross. When the defenders win possession, they try to feed their forwards in the opposition's half, where the same scenario may be repeated.

The objective of this drill is for the defenders to deny space to the forwards, block shots, head crosses and make tackles, and also to try to relieve the pressure by passing to their forwards in the opposition's half. The goalkeeper starts each attack by either feeding his defenders to play out, or throwing directly in to his forward players in the opposition's half.

DEFENSIVE HEADING

In defending high balls, two players – sometimes even three or four – go for the ball. The defender must get his arms up and out to help achieve that extra lift and elevation in order to head the ball from a relatively square position. A one-footed take-off is preferable, as it definitely gives a little more lift, but sometimes the defender has to use a two-footed take-off. To encourage a thrusting action with the head and neck on contact with the ball, you can say to young players: 'With your arms up, helping elevation, put your head through the imaginary picture frame you are holding.'

To practise heading technique, one player can simply throw the ball up for another player to head it. The following drills will provide more realistic, active practices. Note that these practise match situations, and the numbers given to the players here relate to the numbers that would be used in a match proper.

Eyes on the ball and arms raised, the defender attacks the ball, thrusting his head forward to try to gain distance.

Team defending: match situations

These drills duplicate situations all of which could occur in matches. The defending and attacking teams both have clear objectives: the attackers must try to score and the defenders must prevent them by winning the ball and transferring it either into the other half, or to the coach inside the centre circle. If the ball is kicked, headed or tackled out of play, that also counts as a defensive success.

In the first drill (Figure 74a), four defenders (O2, O3, O5 and O6) must clear high balls – pumped in from the right- and left-backs – from the penalty area when they are under pressure from the attacking players. The defenders must 'attack the ball and be first'. If an attacker manages the first header, the other forwards must react. If the ball drops towards midfield, the two defensive midfield players must defend it. This drill must always start with a high ball from the right- or left-back.

Figure 74a

In the second scenario, (Figure 74b) the back four (O2, O3, O5 and O6) stay close together as a unit and the ball starts off in the opponents' half. The defenders should not stand directly behind the attackers and get blocked off, but slightly to one side over one shoulder. For example, the first central defender, O5, should mark over the right shoulder of the centre-forward, 9, giving himself a clear view of the ball and marking 'channel side'. The second centre-half, O6, should mark similarly over the right shoulder of the facing forward, 10.

Figure 74b

In the third drill (Figure 74c), the ball is delivered from well inside the attacking half. In this case, the defenders must stay especially close to their attackers. You will notice that O5 is now marking the attacker, 9, on his left shoulder (goal-side), while O6 and O3 move over into covering postions.

These drills can be varied by changing the delivery. Balls can be fed in to the feet of the front players, or to the feet of the midfield players to feed up to the front. A midfield player can set the ball back to the full-back, who then plays it over the top of the defenders. The full-back can play to the winger, 11's, feet and then support, drawing defenders across.

All the time, we are moving defenders and asking questions of their defensive abilities.

Defending around the box. The defender is marking the forward tightly and goal-side. Note that he is not directly behind but is marking over the forward's left shoulder.

Figure 74c

Defending crosses

In the first drill (Figure 75a), it is assumed that one of the four defenders has been occupied closing down the man with the ball, leaving O5, O6 and O3 to defend against 9, 10 and 7. Defender O5 must mark the space at the near post, O6 must mark the central area and O3 must cover the back post. The three defending players must be well spaced out and able to mark the width of the 6-yard box.

The defenders must be aggressive, brave and really determined to be first to the ball. They are in real trouble if the attackers get the first header or touch. It is worth reminding them that the starting positions are just that: if the defenders fail to attack the ball, the forwards will. Once the ball is in motion, the defenders should adjust to deal with the different types of cross and not just the runs of the attackers.

In the second drill (Figure 75b), the winger, player 11, has been forced by defender O2 to check back on to his right foot. The cross is now bent inwards to the central/far-post area. This delaying by defender O2 allows the other defenders a snatch of time to move out, trying to catch the forwards offside.

In both these drills, the underlying philosophy – which bears repetition – is that when the ball comes into the box defending players must make the first header or contact with the ball. Don't worry who you are marking: *attack the ball!*

Opposite: *Marking positions from a cross. As the cross is about to be delivered, the defenders in the penalty area are well spaced out from each other. These positions aim to cover most situations: it is then a matter of attacking the ball as it is crossed in.*

Figure 75a

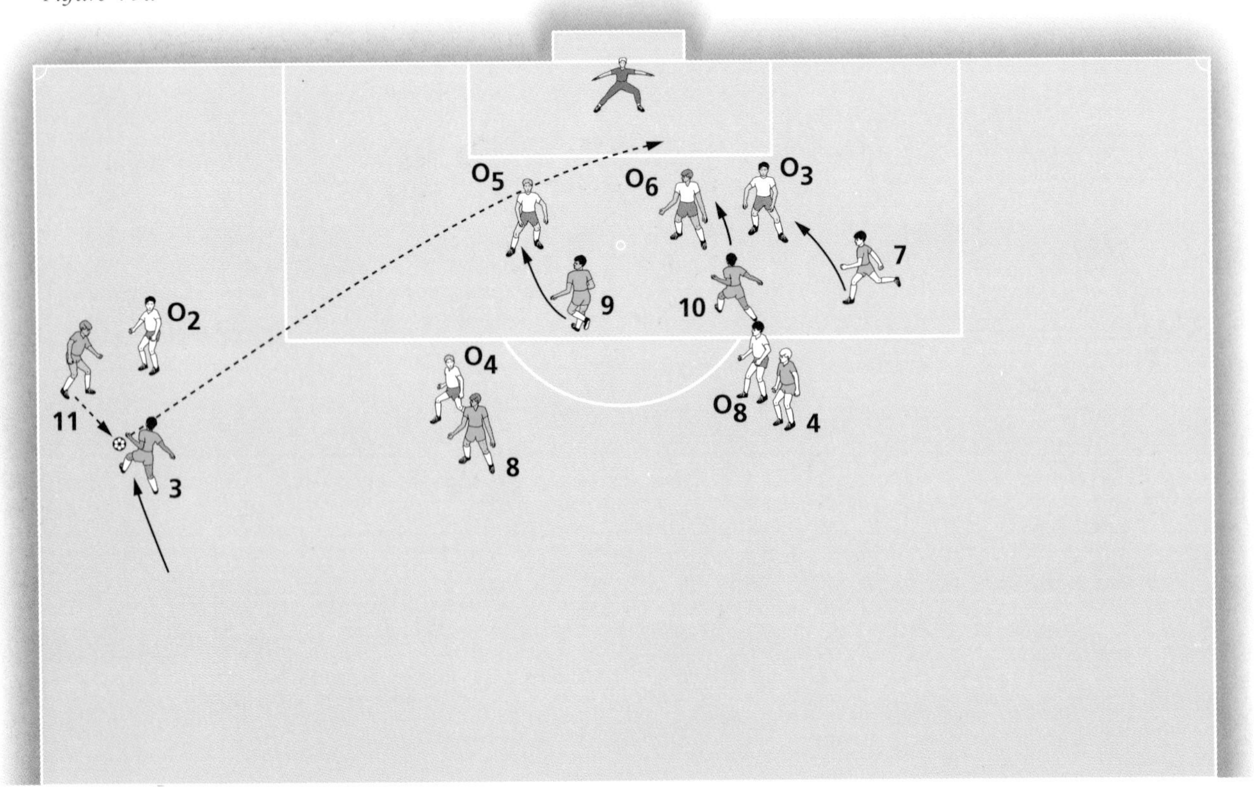

CARLING
NORTHERN ROCK
SPORTS
NORTHERN ROCK
DAGENHAM MOTORS
CARLING
DAGENHAM MOTORS
8

Figure 75b

O5
O6
O3
7
O2
11
9
10
O4
O8
3
8
4

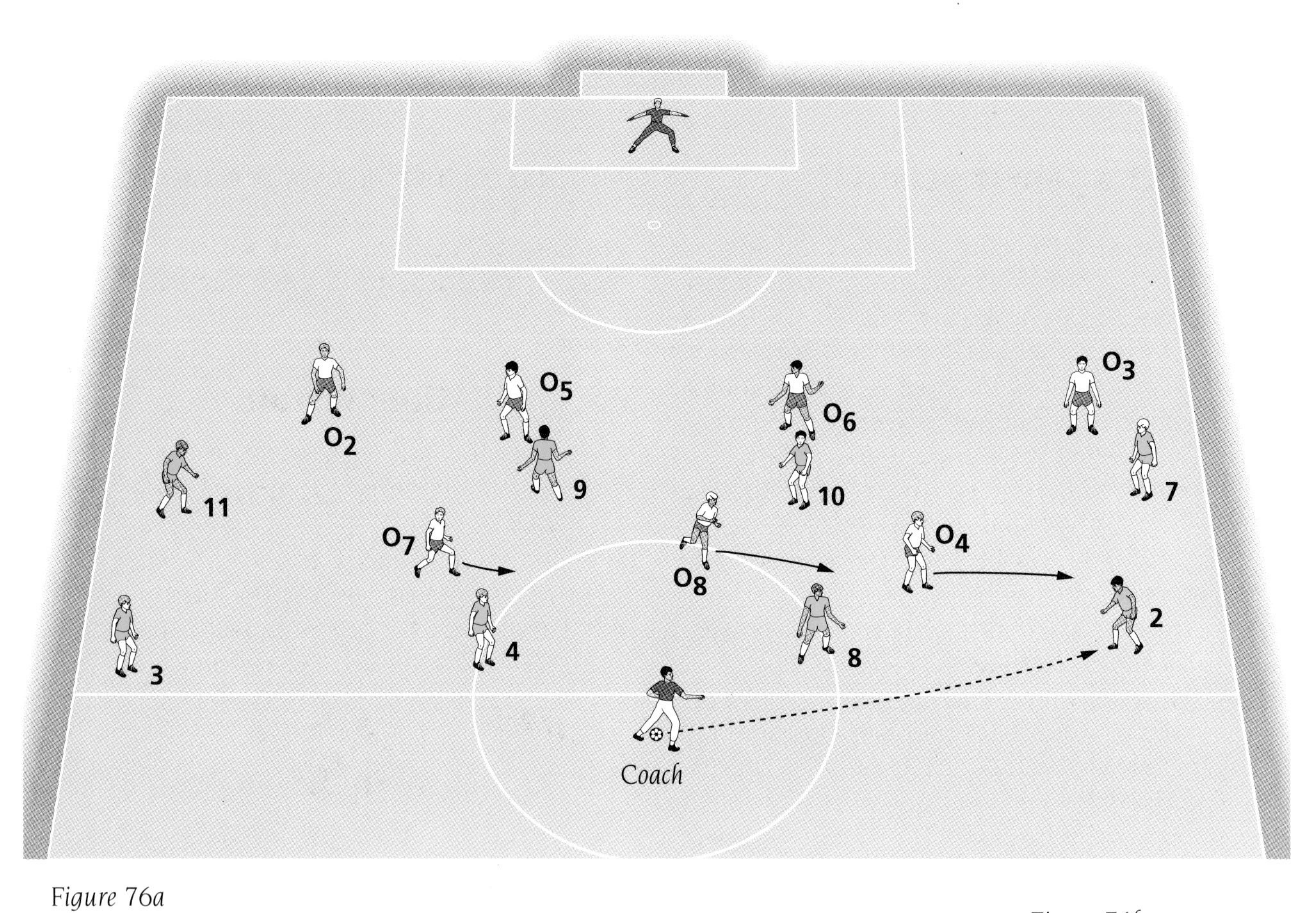

Figure 76a

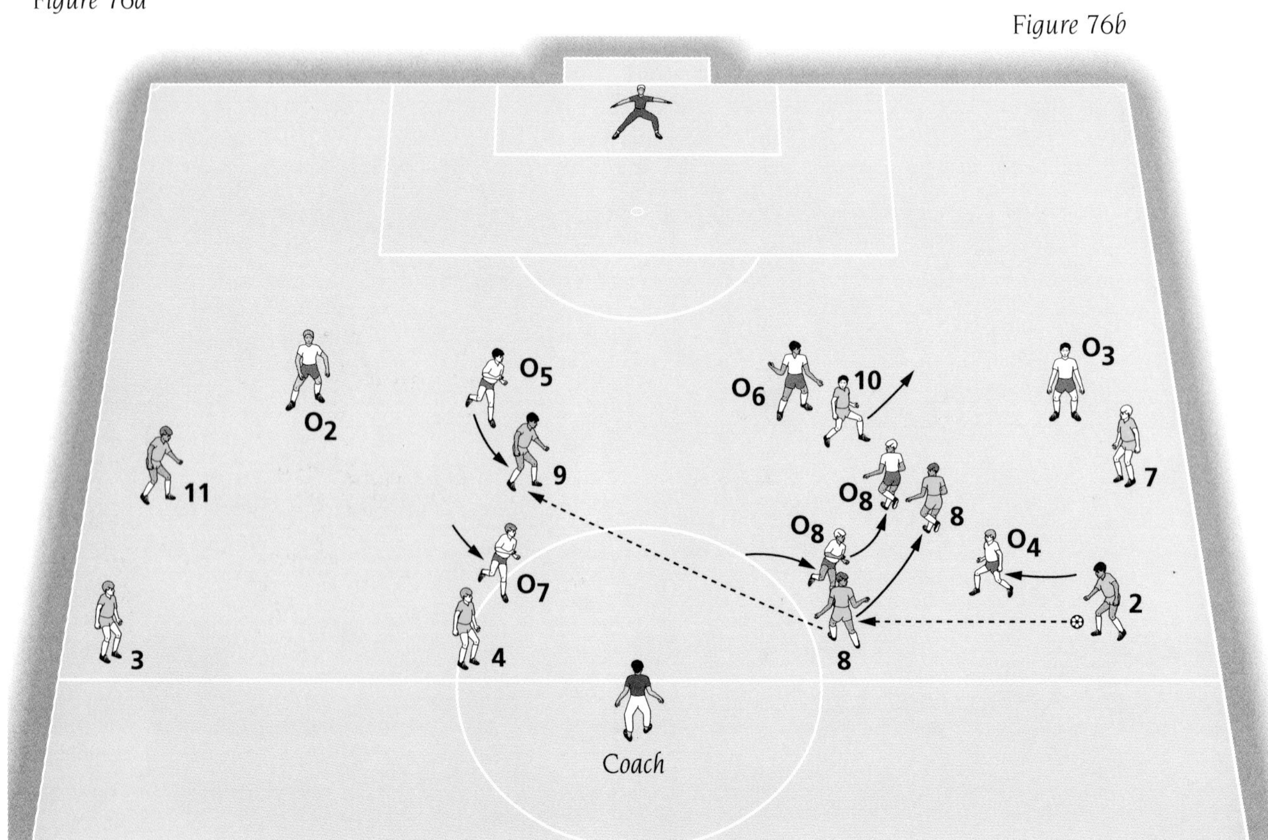

Figure 76b

Eight against seven

In these drills, a defensive back four mark four forwards (two wingers and two central strikers), and a defensive midfield three play against a midfield four (two midfield players and two attacking full-backs), making it eight against seven, plus a goalkeeper.

In the first drill (Figure 76a), player 2 is given possession, so the defending midfielders O4, O8, and O7 have to move across, leaving 3, the left-back, who is no real threat, free.

In the second drill (Figure 76b), player 2 passes to 8. Defenders O4 and O8 must move to close down the passing option. If player 8 passes to 9, the back four and O5 come into play, while if 9 finds 3 (Figure 76c) with the ball the defenders must adjust again, with O7 going to the ball and O4 filling the space. Note that in both situations O8 has tracked 8's forward run.

Playing out these scenarios will teach players the discipline of defending as a unit.

Conclusion

Delaying attackers is important. Defending must be disciplined, particularly in one-against-one situations, and also has to be carried out as a group. You should encourage the wholehearted, 100 per cent approach to defending.

Figure 76c

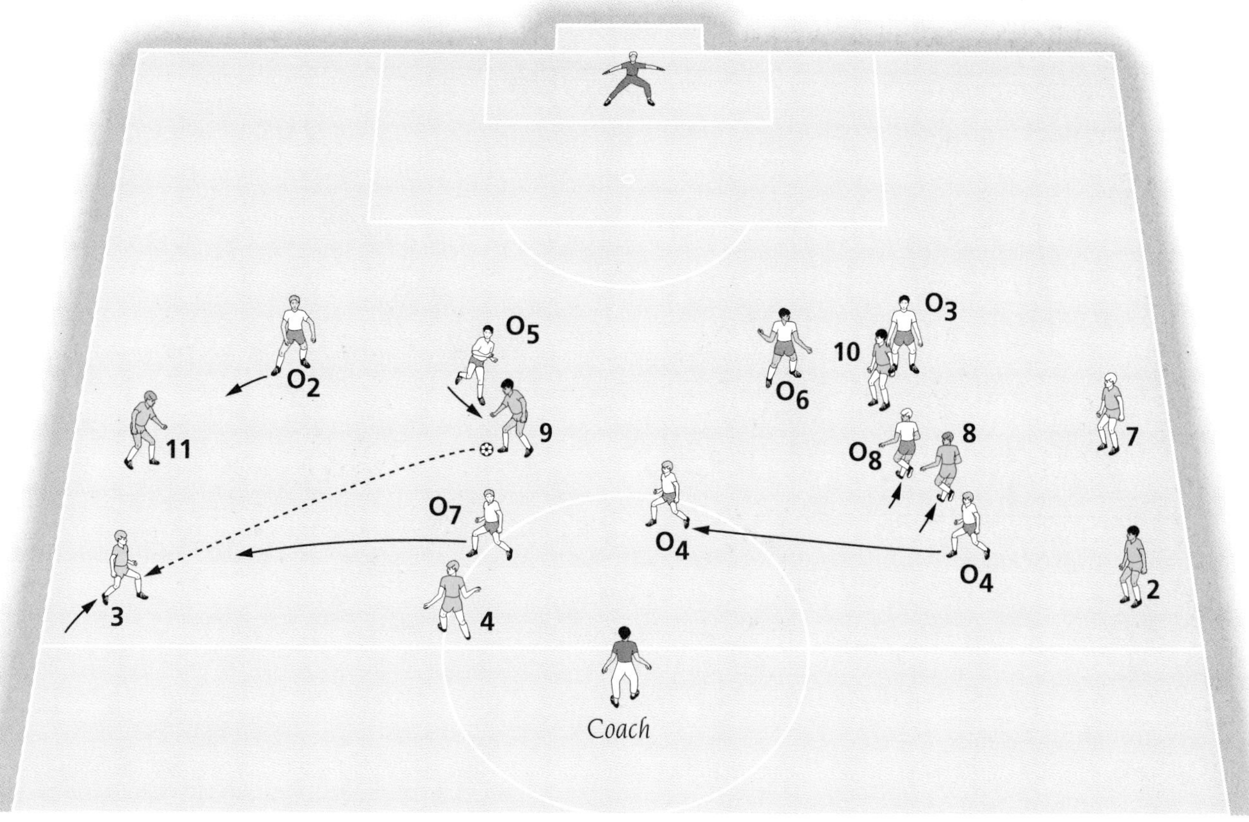

CARLING

CARLING

8
COACHING TOWARDS A BETTER FUTURE

IN THE BRITISH game, we have in the past displayed a poor understanding of patience when building attacks and have failed to produce players who are technically gifted in every department. The transfer system has been going through massive changes, and with regulations and boundaries breaking down throughout Europe, and indeed the world, the Klinsmanns, Ginolas, Viallis and Juninhos are coming into the British game and opening coaches' eyes to the fact that they have been educated differently. Their skills look so natural, yet essentially they have been *coached* to do it naturally. I firmly believe that the British coaching system has to copy the best of what other countries have to offer and improve upon it. This will produce players for future generations who are not so rigid in their approach and will be tagged 'footballers', rather than players who play in a set position – full-back, centre-half, centre-forward and so on.

In order to learn from the Continentals, coaches need to accept that they in turn have learned from the British game. While English clubs dominated European competitions in the late 1970s and early 1980s, foreign coaches recognized the English sides' organizational strengths and added the natural English determination and spirit to their own game. They realized that they had to compete physically and now produce more athletic footballers, without sacrificing brilliant technical and tactical understanding. If the British game is to take foreign ideas on board and bring them into the national game, there will have to be a fundamental rethink of the overall approach.

In the Premiership, the youth policies of Manchester United and Liverpool (which include both recruitment *and* coaching) are bearing fruit in terms of success on the pitch, and this is reviving belief in the importance of youth development nationally. For West Ham United, the emphasis we place on producing our own young players and playing the 'West Ham Way' is, today, just as important as it was during the 1960s, 1970s and 1980s, when Ron Greenwood and John Lyall were the managers.

INDEX